SignalR – Real-time Application Development

Second Edition

A fast-paced guide to develop, test, and deliver real-time communication in your .NET applications using SignalR

Einar Ingebrigtsen

[PACKT] open source *
PUBLISHING   community experience distilled

BIRMINGHAM - MUMBAI

SignalR – Real-time Application Development

Second Edition

First published: June 2013

Second edition: September 2015

Production reference: 1240915

Published by Packt Publishing Ltd.
Livery Place
35 Livery Street
Birmingham B3 2PB, UK.

ISBN 978-1-78528-545-5

www.packtpub.com

Credits

Author
Einar Ingebrigtsen

Reviewers
Niclas Sahlin
Najam Uddin

Commissioning Editor
Dipika Gaonkar

Acquisition Editors
Vinay Argekar
Sam Wood

Content Development Editor
Rashmi Suvarna

Technical Editor
Madhunikita Sunil Chindarkar

Copy Editor
Trishya Hajare

Project Coordinator
Judie Jose

Proofreader
Safis Editing

Indexer
Priya Sane

Production Coordinator
Nitesh Thakur

Cover Work
Nitesh Thakur

About the Author

Einar Ingebrigtsen has been working professionally with software since 1994 — ranging from games development on platforms such as PlayStation, Xbox, and the PC to the enterprise line of business application development since 2002. He has always focused on creating great products with great user experiences, putting the user first. Einar was a Microsoft MVP awardee from October 2008 until July 2015, which he was awarded for his work in the community and in the Silverlight space with open source projects such as Balder, a 3D engine for Silverlight. For years, Einar ran a company called Dolittle together with partners, doing consultancy work and building their own products with their own open source projects at the heart of what they did. Amongst the clients that Dolittle has had over the last couple of years include NRK (the largest TV broadcaster in Norway), Statoil (a Norwegian oil company), Komplett (the largest e-commerce company in Norway), and Holte (a leading Norwegian developer for construction software). Today, Einar works for Microsoft as a technical evangelist, focusing on Azure and advising ISVs, which meant giving up the MVP title.

A strong believer in open source, he runs a few projects in addition to Balder, the largest being Bifrost (`http://bifr.st`), a line of business platforms for .NET developers, and also worth mentioning is Forseti (`http://github.com/dolittle/forseti`), a headless auto-running JavaScript test runner.

Additionally, Einar loves talking at user groups and conferences and has been a frequent speaker at Microsoft venues, talking about different topics — the last couple of years he has mostly focused on architecture, code quality, and cloud computing.

His personal blog is at `http://www.ingebrigtsen.info`.

Einar has also published another book on the subject of *SignalR Blueprints*, by Packt Publishing.

Acknowledgments

It might sound like a cliché, but seriously, without my wife Anne Grethe this book could not have happened. Her patience with me and her support is truly what pretty much makes just about anything I do turn into a reality. To my kids, Mia and Herman, you rock! Thanks to my kids for keeping me mentally younger and playful. I'd also like to thank my colleagues, who have been kind enough to not point out that I've had too much going on in the period of writing this book. I'll be sure to buy a round the next time we're having a company get-together.

About the Reviewers

Niclas Sahlin works as a software developer in Gothenburg, Sweden. After graduating from Chalmers University of Technology with a degree in software engineering in 2012, he started working full-time with ASP.NET, and has not turned his back on it since.

His first contact with ASP.NET was during his studies at Chalmers. He used it in various projects in his spare time and soon took interest in the frontend side of web development. During the development of a game together with two friends, he discovered SignalR and the capabilities the library provided, and he has used it for many projects since then.

You can find Niclas on Twitter as `@niclassahlin` or visit his blog at `www.niclassahlin.com` to learn more about him and what he does.

Najam Uddin specializes in designing and creating secure and scalable solutions. With over 10 years of experience in software design, development, and support, he has engineered strong, data-driven web applications and services for the banking and finance, oil and gas, and insurance industries. He is mainly focused on the Microsoft technology stack. He has a master of science degree from Birla Institute of Technology and Science, Pilani. You can contact him at `connect@najam.in`.

www.PacktPub.com

Support files, eBooks, discount offers, and more

For support files and downloads related to your book, please visit www.PacktPub.com.

Did you know that Packt offers eBook versions of every book published, with PDF and ePub files available? You can upgrade to the eBook version at www.PacktPub.com and as a print book customer, you are entitled to a discount on the eBook copy. Get in touch with us at service@packtpub.com for more details.

At www.PacktPub.com, you can also read a collection of free technical articles, sign up for a range of free newsletters and receive exclusive discounts and offers on Packt books and eBooks.

https://www2.packtpub.com/books/subscription/packtlib

Do you need instant solutions to your IT questions? PacktLib is Packt's online digital book library. Here, you can search, access, and read Packt's entire library of books.

Why subscribe?

- Fully searchable across every book published by Packt
- Copy and paste, print, and bookmark content
- On demand and accessible via a web browser

Free access for Packt account holders

If you have an account with Packt at www.PacktPub.com, you can use this to access PacktLib today and view 9 entirely free books. Simply use your login credentials for immediate access.

Table of Contents

Preface   **v**

Chapter 1: The Primer   **1**

Where are we coming from?   2
    The terminal   2
    Fast forwarding   3
    Completing the circle   4
    SignalR   6

Terminology   7
    Messaging   7
    Publish/subscribe   7
    Decoupling   8

Patterns   10
    Model View Controller   10
    Model View ViewModel   12

Libraries and frameworks   13
    jQuery   14
    ASP.NET MVC 5   14
    AngularJS   15
    Twitter Bootstrap   15

Tools   **15**
    Visual Studio 2013   15
    NuGet   16

Summary   **19**

Chapter 2: Persistent Connections   **21**

Persistent connections – what are they?   **21**
Where are we going?   **22**
Getting the project ready   **22**
Setting up the packages   24
The single page application   25
The "code-behind"   28
Getting started with the server-side   **30**
Connecting the dots   31
Making the UI light up   33
Summary   **35**

Chapter 3: Hubs   **37**

Moving up a level   **37**
The client   **40**
Decoupling it all   **40**
The Dependency Inversion Principle   42
Proxies   42
Life cycle events   **46**
Separation   **47**
Summary   **47**

Chapter 4: Groups   **49**

Getting specific with groups   **49**
Composing the UI   **54**
Summary   **62**

Chapter 5: State   **63**

Becoming stateful   **63**
The client   65
Lifetime event handlers and more   67
Summary   **67**

Chapter 6: Security   **69**

Locking things down   **69**
Putting the infrastructure in place   **70**
HTTP handler config   **71**
Authentication   **73**
Securing the hub   **80**
The great finale   **81**
Summary   **82**

Chapter 7: Scaling Out   83
It's all about messages in SignalR   83
Scaling out with SQL Server   84
Scaling out with Redis   86
Scaling out with Azure   87
Creating our own backplane   90
Hooking it all up   92
Summary   93
Chapter 8: Building a WPF .NET Client   95
Decoupling it all   95
Decoupling – the next level   97
Building for the desktop   98
Setting up the packages   99
Observables   100
Adding security   102
Adding support for cookies   102
Binding helper   103
Creating a client security service   105
Adding a login view   107
The hub proxy   110
Our chat rooms   114
The chat   117
The composition   120
Summary   123
Chapter 9: Write Once, Deploy Many   125
Cross platform   125
Getting started   126
Code signing   131
Preparing for connections   134
Packages   137
MVVM   137
Messenger   138
DelegateCommand   139
Security   144
ChatHub   146
Login   148
ChatRooms   153
Chat   155
The result   158
Summary   160

Chapter 10: Monitoring — 161

Logging — 161
Logging on the server side — 162
Logging in the JavaScript client — 167
Logging in the .NET client — 168
Logging from the Xamarin client — 169
Digging deeper into the communication — 170
Looking under the cover with Fiddler — 171
Performance counters — 172
Under the cover, inside the browser — 177
Summary — 178

Chapter 11: Hosting a Server Using Self-hosted OWIN — 179

Self-hosting — 179
Adding the needed packages — 180
Adding the code needed for self-hosting — 181
The client — 184
Summary — 187

Index — 189

Preface

This preface gives you a look at what this book consists of, conventions and details about downloading, and more. In addition, it establishes a common understanding, setting the theme for the rest of the book. It walks you through the history of application development, especially that of web applications.

The topics that will be covered are as follows:

- Why we need to think differently about our applications and how they relate to a server
- The different techniques that can be used without something like SignalR
- The protocols and techniques that SignalR uses to do what it does
- Why we need something like SignalR
- What UX improvements one could have in an application when applying SignalR

At this stage, the developer should have a basic knowledge of how SignalR works and what the developer needs to rethink when designing applications that have a persistent connection to the server.

The emperor's new clothes

As with fashion, it sometimes feels like history repeats itself in our industry as well. It seems that we have come full circle with how software should be architected. I guess this comes from having pretty much the same goal; software solutions that are available to a lot of users and keep the data as updated as possible for all users. What this means is that we probably want to have a shared data source from where all clients can get their data. It also means that we need some kind of network connection for the clients to connect to the centralized data source. The clients are typically distributed across multiple offices, maybe even different geo-locations. With different geo-locations often comes the challenge of different network types and bandwidth.

The good old terminal

Before we get in to the cool stuff, it's important to gain some perspective on the problem we're trying to solve. It is, in fact, a real problem dating back to the early days of computers.

Back in the 1970s, in the early days of computers, it was quite common to see terminals in offices much like the one shown in the following image:

The nature of these terminals was to be as dumb as possible. They didn't do any computation, nor did they hold any state. The terminal only reflected what the server wanted the terminal to show on screen, so in many ways they were just really fancy television sets. Any input from the user's keyboard was sent to the server, and the server interpreted the user input, updated the users' terminal session, and sent the screen update back to the terminal, as shown in the following diagram:

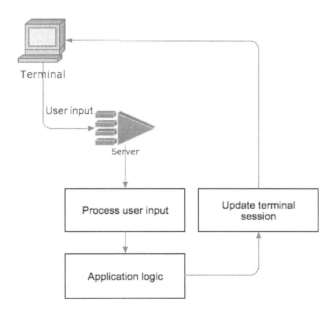

This model proved very helpful; technically, we, as developers, had everything on our server and didn't have to think about any rich clients holding stakes and making it all the more complex. We only needed to scale the server, and potentially deal with multiple servers and keep them in sync, or work against a centralized data source. However, it didn't prove useful for a good user experience. The terminals were limited to text only, and the types of user interface one could create were limited, often ending up being very data-centric and keyboard-friendly.

X Server

The X Window system (commonly known as X11) came in 1984, originating at the Massachusetts Institute of Technology (MIT). It was a graphical user interface system. With it came a network protocol to enable networked computers to connect to servers in a similar fashion as the terminals of the '70s, but, with its graphical capabilities, it was a big step up from the text-based terminal.

As with the terminal solution, the users' input was to be sent to a server, and the software the user used would, in fact, run on that very server. The result in the graphical user interface would then be sent back to the client machine, as represented in the following figure, again leaving the client to be rather dumb and passive:

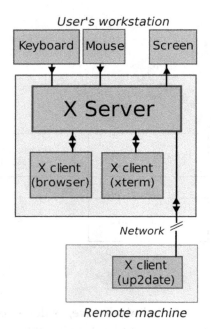

Remote desktop

Meanwhile, in the world of Windows, in 1998, Windows NT 4.0 got a new edition of the operating system: *Terminal Server Edition*. With this edition, Microsoft introduced a new protocol called the Remote Desktop Protocol (RDP). It enabled the client to view another computer's desktop. With NT4 Terminal Server, the operating system was able to host multiple desktops for multiple users at the same time. From this remote desktop, clients could then launch any application they wanted that existed on the server they were connected to. As with the good old terminals, the client computer did not need to be very capable. In fact, this turned out to give birth to an industry, Think Client computers, capable of connecting to RDP-enabled servers, as shown in the following block diagram:

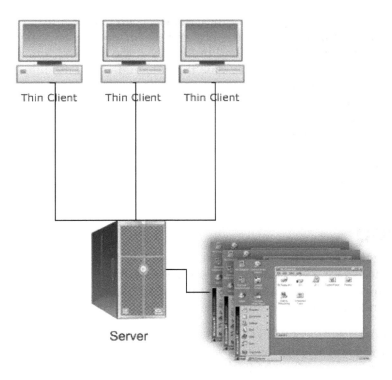

Rich clients

Running the software on the server puts tremendous pressure on the server and its capability. The server must be capable of handling all the users and their inputs, which leads to the need for a certain computational power; of course, depending upon the application itself.

Sometimes it does not make any sense to have everything running on a server. It might not be worth it for your particular application, or it might be too costly to try to scale for what you need. It can also be a question of responsiveness; your app might need more responsiveness to make sense to the user. However, taking the step into the world of a rich stateful client normally increases the complexity of our solutions, depending on what we're making.

If we do not have any concurrency issues or data that has become stale, we don't necessarily have any issues that need to be solved. Unfortunately, for most lines of business software out there, this is not the case. We need to take into consideration that there might be multiple users out there, and decide on how to deal with them. We can go down the optimistic path and pretend that the users seldom run into each other's data and we just overwrite any data that we might have modified while we were making a change in the same piece of data. We could also go pessimistic and not allow that at all, which would give us an exceptional state in the application that we often let our users deal with. This way, we can let the rich clients deal with this and pretty much leave the problem behind and use something like TCP sockets and communicate among the clients as they are changing the state. The other respective clients can then pick up the change and alter their own state before the user saves theirs. They can even notify the user that someone else has modified it.

The Web

Here we are again, back to the dumb client. Our web browsers have served as the passive client for years. The model is frighteningly similar to the terminal solution of the '70s; a dumb client capable of taking input and rendering whatever comes across the network, and a rich server doing all the work.

Hypertext Transfer Protocol (HTTP) is what makes up the Web. It surfaced for the first time in 1991 and basically describes a protocol for making a request to a server and the server sending a response back. The protocol is stateless and you will need to keep the state either on the server or the client. Within the protocol there are well-defined verbs that can be used, such as POST, GET, PUT, DELETE, and many more. These verbs let us describe what we are doing. However, a well-defined and rich protocol has nothing defined in it to let the clients be persistently connected. You can read more about HTTP at `http://en.wikipedia.org/wiki/Http`.

As the capability of web browsers has increased over time, we've watched them go from being very passive to rich clients. The mid 2000s gave us the buzz often referred to as Web 2.0 and AJAX (Asynchronous JavaScript and XML). At the core of this JavaScript was something called XHR (XMLHttpRequest), making it programmatically possible to call the server from the client without any user interaction. This technique leverages HTTP, and you find yourself getting parts or even the data instead of getting whole web pages. You can put the data into the already-rendered web page. You can find more details about AJAX at `http://en.wikipedia.org/wiki/Ajax_(programming)`.

Modern web applications are turning into a hybrid of rich clients and thin clients; very capable, but they shouldn't do it all – we also need the server-side logic. A true step in the right direction is letting the client be good at its forte and doing likewise with the server, thus separating the concerns of the two tiers.

Now that we have all this power in the browser, we quickly run into similar problems as those we run into with regular rich clients, that is, states on the client.

Full duplex on the Web

With the evolution going back to where we started from, meaning that we are now at a point where we need the same kind of connectivity that we needed for rich desktop applications in the past, but now the demand is that applications go live on the web. With user demand come technical challenges: the web is not built for this; the web is based on a request/response pattern. The browser goes to a specific URL and a server generates a resource.

One of the things that the W3C organization has done to accommodate this need is the standardization of something called WebSocket: full-duplex communication channel over a single TCP connection. A very good initiative is something that will be supported by all browser vendors as well as web servers. The challenge, with it getting a broad adoption, is on the infrastructure that makes up the Web. The entire infrastructure has been optimized for the request/response pattern, and a steady connection establishes a point-to-point connection between two computers, and all of a sudden scalability becomes an issue. So in many cases, this might not be the best solution.

Events

Another initiative called server-sent events was implemented by Opera, the Norwegian browser vendor, which is now being standardized by W3C. It gives us the opportunity to push events from the server to the clients that are connected. On combining it with the regular HTTP request/response, we are able to meet the requirements of rich applications. You can read more about server-sent events at `http://en.wikipedia.org/wiki/Server-sent_events`.

Comet

Not changing the subject just yet, a technique called Comet has also been applied with great success. The basic principle is to utilize something called long polling HTTP requests. One opens an HTTP request to the server from the client, and the server does not return anything until it has something to return, like an event that happens on the server. When the response has been given, the client starts a new long polling connection and keeps on doing so for ever. This simulates a full-duplex connection and scales very well with the existing infrastructure of the Web, as shown in the following block diagram. You can read more about comet here: `http://en.wikipedia.org/wiki/Comet_(programming)`.

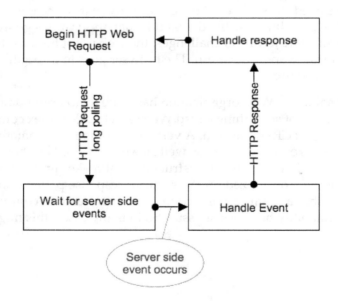

Hand-rolling it all

By now you probably know where I am going with this. The techniques described previously are some of the techniques that SignalR utilizes. The techniques and standards are well known, and nothing is holding you back from working with them directly, but this is where SignalR comes in and saves the day.

Why?

The most important thing to ask in software development is "why?" (http://en.wikipedia.org/wiki/5_Whys). Why do we want all this? What is it that we're really trying to solve? We're trying to make the software more collaborative and make users work together without having artificial technical limitations to this collaboration. In fact, why not have the changes occur in real time when all the users are collaborating?

Now what?

SignalR represents an abstraction for all the techniques that it supports today, and with it we also gain the extensibility of supporting techniques that might come along in the future. It has a built-in fallback mechanism which enables it to pick the best solution for your app and its environment, and it is also based on the client connection. In addition, SignalR provides great mechanisms for scaling out in a multiserver environment, enabling applications to be blissfully unaware of the server they are running on and just work with the same abstraction as if it was only one server.

Think different

Apple coined the phrase *Think different* back in 1997. The phrase in itself forces you to think differently, since it is grammatically incorrect. With all the asynchronous operations and events going into a technology like SignalR, one really has to think in a different manner, but a manner that is different in a good way. It is good for users, as we are now forced to create user experiences that are non-blocking. Of course, you as a developer can force locks onto the users, but I would argue that it would be easier not to, and instead approach building the user interface in a different manner.

For instance, one of the things that we tend to build into our apps is the notion of concurrency and stale data. We don't want to run the risk of two users updating the exact same data and one client not having the updated data from the other user. Often we leave our users to get a bizarre error message that the user often won't understand. A better solution would be to have all the data on all user screens be updated as they are looking at it, and maybe even make them aware in a subtle way of the changes that happened due to the other user(s).

Personal style

Throughout this book, you'll run into things you might disagree with. It could be things in naming the classes or methods in C#, for instance, at times, I like to drop camel casing, both upper and lower, and just separate the words with underscores yielding "some_type_with_spaces". In addition, I don't use modifiers without them adding any value. You'll see that I completely avoid private as that is the default modifier for fields or properties on types. I'll also avoid things such as read-only, especially if it's a private member. Most annoyingly, you might see that I drop scoping for single line statements following an *IF* or *FOR*. Don't worry, this is my personal style; you can do as you please. All I'm asking is that you don't judge me by how my code looks. I'm not a huge fan of measuring code quality with tools such as R# and its default setting for squiggles. In fact, a colleague and I have been toying with the idea of using the underscore trick for all our code, as it really makes it a lot easier to read.

You'll notice throughout that I'm using built-in functions in the browser in JavaScript, where you might expect jQuery. The reason for this is basically that I try to limit the usage of jQuery. In fact, it's a dependency I'd prefer not to have in my solutions, as it does not add anything to the way I do things. There is a bit of an educational, also quite intentional, reason for me to not use jQuery as well: we now have most of the things we need in the browser already.

What this book covers

Chapter 1, The Primer, explains that in order to get started with SignalR and real-time web applications, it is important to understand the motivation behind wanting to have such a technology and way of approaching application development.

Chapter 2, Persistent Connections, explains that at the core of SignalR sits something called PersistentConnection, and this is where everything starts. In this chapter, you will learn how to get started with it on the backend and consume it in the frontend.

Chapter 3, Hubs, enables us to move from persistent connections to one abstraction up: something called hubs. A hub provides a more natural abstraction for most scenarios. They are easier to write and easier to consume.

Chapter 4, Groups, explains that sometimes you want to filter messages so that you have better control over which client gets which messages. Grouping in SignalR is a way to accomplish this. You will learn how to deal with this on the server and the client.

Chapter 5, State, explains that in addition to sending messages between clients and servers that are very explicit, you sometimes need to have accompanying metadata or additional data that is cross-cutting. In this chapter, you will learn about states that can go back and forth with messages.

Chapter 6, Security, explains that just about any application needs to take security into consideration. In this chapter, you will learn techniques you can apply to your SignalR code to secure messages.

Chapter 7, Scaling Out, explains that building applications that scale on multiple servers can be a bit of a puzzle. This chapter will show you how to scale out and be able to deal with these, both in an on-premise environment and in Microsoft's Windows Azure cloud.

Chapter 8, Building a WPF .NET Client, explains that SignalR is not only for web applications. It can be utilized with great success in other client types as well. This chapter shows you how to build a desktop client for Windows using WPF and .NET.

Chapter 9, Write Once, Deploy Many, takes SignalR even further, beyond both the Web and desktop to the mobile space. In this chapter, you will learn how to take your SignalR knowledge and expand into areas like iOS, Android, and Windows Phone.

Chapter 10, Monitoring, explains that debugging is a part of everyday life as a developer, and this, of course, applies to development with SignalR too. This chapter will show you how to monitor messages and look at possible performance bottlenecks.

Chapter 11, Hosting a Server Using Self-hosted OWIN, explains that open web interfaces for .NET are an abstraction enabling web frameworks to be agnostic about the underlying platform. In this chapter, we will look at how to self-host in a simple console application using OWIN.

What you need for this book

The book uses C# and JavaScript in the samples, and we will use Visual Studio 2013 as the IDE of choice. You will also be able to use Visual Studio 2013 Community edition, which is the free edition. You will need to have NuGet installed, which can be accessed at http://www.nuget.org. For the Xamarin part of this book, you will need to have access to a Mac with XCode installed, plus Xamarin Studio, which you can download at http://www.xamarin.com. Xamarin does provide a plugin for Visual Studio, but it needs to work in conjunction with a tool running on Mac OS X that compiles the code for use on iOS and also runs it either on iOS Simulator or a real device.

Who this book is for

This book is written for developers with experience in C# and JavaScript. At this stage, the developer should also have a basic knowledge of how SignalR works, as well as what the developer needs to rethink when designing applications that have a persistent connection to the server.

Some of the things that we will be discussing in the book are architectural in nature. Software architecture, patterns, and practices surround us, and this book will present some less "mainstream" ideas that are ideal for the world of small changes. You don't need to be an architect to get this; the book will keep it at an intermediate level.

Conventions

In this book, you will find a number of text styles that distinguish between different kinds of information. Here are some examples of these styles and an explanation of their meaning.

Code words in text, database table names, folder names, filenames, file extensions, path names, dummy URLs, user input, and Twitter handles are shown as follows: "At the core level of SignalR sits something called a PersistentConnection class; hubs build on top of this."

A block of code is set as follows:

```
function someFunctionDoingSomething() {
   // It should perform some work
}
```

Any command-line input or output is written as follows:

```
install-package <package-name> -version <package-version>
```

New terms and **important words** are shown in bold. Words that you see on the screen, for example, in menus or dialog boxes, appear in the text like this: "With the code running, you should now see a **Started** message in the console of the developer tool."

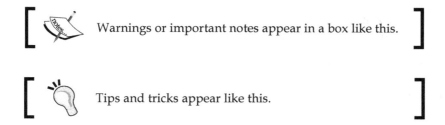

Warnings or important notes appear in a box like this.

Tips and tricks appear like this.

Reader feedback

Feedback from our readers is always welcome. Let us know what you think about this book—what you liked or disliked. Reader feedback is important for us as it helps us develop titles that you will really get the most out of.

To send us general feedback, simply e-mail feedback@packtpub.com, and mention the book's title in the subject of your message.

If there is a topic that you have expertise in and you are interested in either writing or contributing to a book, see our author guide at www.packtpub.com/authors.

Customer support

Now that you are the proud owner of a Packt book, we have a number of things to help you to get the most from your purchase.

Downloading the example code

You can download the example code files from your account at http://www.packtpub.com for all the Packt Publishing books you have purchased. If you purchased this book elsewhere, you can visit http://www.packtpub.com/support and register to have the files e-mailed directly to you.

Errata

Although we have taken every care to ensure the accuracy of our content, mistakes do happen. If you find a mistake in one of our books—maybe a mistake in the text or the code—we would be grateful if you could report this to us. By doing so, you can save other readers from frustration and help us improve subsequent versions of this book. If you find any errata, please report them by visiting `http://www.packtpub.com/submit-errata`, selecting your book, clicking on the **Errata Submission Form** link, and entering the details of your errata. Once your errata are verified, your submission will be accepted and the errata will be uploaded to our website or added to any list of existing errata under the Errata section of that title.

To view the previously submitted errata, go to `https://www.packtpub.com/books/content/support` and enter the name of the book in the search field. The required information will appear under the **Errata** section.

Piracy

Piracy of copyrighted material on the Internet is an ongoing problem across all media. At Packt, we take the protection of our copyright and licenses very seriously. If you come across any illegal copies of our works in any form on the Internet, please provide us with the location address or website name immediately so that we can pursue a remedy.

Please contact us at `copyright@packtpub.com` with a link to the suspected pirated material.

We appreciate your help in protecting our authors and our ability to bring you valuable content.

Questions

If you have a problem with any aspect of this book, you can contact us at `questions@packtpub.com`, and we will do our best to address the problem.

1
The Primer

This chapter serves as a primer of knowledge. With this, you will become aware of all the terms, patterns, and practices applied in the book. Also, you will learn about the tools, libraries, and frameworks being used and what their use cases are. More importantly, you will find out why you should be performing these different things and, in particular, why you are using SignalR, and how the methods you employ will naturally find their way into your software.

In this chapter, the following topics will be covered:

- Walk-through architectural patterns
- Messaging — what is it?
- Publish/subscribe models
- Decoupling for scale — why and how?
- Frontend patterns — also back to decoupling
  - MVC
  - MVVM
- AngularJS
- Twitter Bootstrap — using it to make things look better
- SignalR — what is it built of and how does it all come together?

Where are we coming from?

By asking where are we coming from, I'm not trying to ask an existential question that dates back to the first signs of life on this planet. Rather, we are looking at the scope of our industry, and what has directed us all the way to where we are now and how we create software today. The software industry is very young and is constantly moving. We haven't quite settled in yet like other professions have. The rapid advances in computer hardware present opportunities for software all the time. We find better ways of doing things as we improve our skills as a community. With the Internet and the means of communication that we have today, these changes are happening fast and frequently. This is to say that collectively, we are changing a lot more than any other industry. With all this being said, a lot of these changes go back to the roots of our industry. They seek back as if we could now do things right as they were intended in the first place, only in a slightly modified version with a few new techniques or perspectives. Computers and software are the tools meant to solve problems for humans, and often in the line of business applications that we write; these tools and software are there to remove manual labor or remove paper clutter. The way these applications are modeled is therefore often closely related to the manual or paper version, not really modeling the process or applying the full capability of what the computer could do to actually improve the experience of the particular process.

The terminal

Back in the early days of computing, computers lacked CPU power and memory. They were expensive, and if you wanted something powerful, it would fill the room with refrigerator-sized computers. The idea of a computer on each desk, at least a powerful one, was not feasible. Instead of delivering rich computers onto desks, the notion of terminals became a reality. These were connected to the mainframe and were completely stateless.

The entirety of each terminal was kept in the mainframe, and the only thing transferred from the client was user input and the only thing coming back from the mainframe was any screen updates.

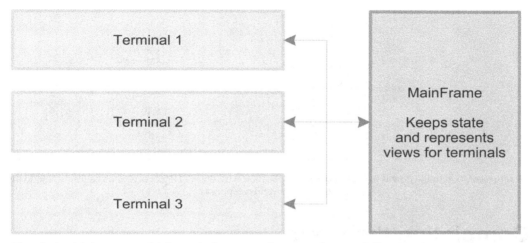

The relationship between multiple terminals connected to a mainframe and all terminals exist without state, with the mainframe maintaining the state and views

Fast forwarding

The previous methods of thinking established the pattern for software moving through the decades. If you look at web applications with a server component in the early days of the Web, you'll see the exact same pattern: a server that keeps the state of the user and the clients being pretty less; this being the web browser. In fact, the only thing going back and forth between them was the user input from the client and the result in the form of HTML going back.

Bringing this image really up to speed with the advancement of AJAX, the image would be represented as shown in the following diagram:

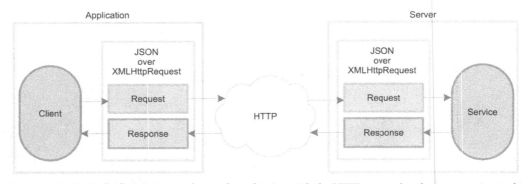

A representation to the flow is in a modern web application with the HTTP protocol and requests going to the server that yields responses

Completing the circle

Of course, by skipping three decades of evolution in computing, we are bound to miss a few things. However, the gist of most techniques has been that we keep the state on the server and we have to go from the client in the sense of request, be it a keystroke or a HTTP request, before receiving a response. At the core of this sits a network stack with capabilities beyond what the overlying techniques have been doing. In games, for instance, the underlying sockets have been used much more in order for us to be able to actually play multiplayer games, starting off with games on your local network to massive multiplayer online games with thousands of users connected at once. In games, the request/response pattern will not work as they yield different techniques and patterns. We can't apply all the things that have been achieved in games because a lot of it is based on approximation due to network latency. However, we don't have the requirements of games either to reflect the truth in an interval of every 16-20 milliseconds. Accuracy is far more important in the world of line of business application development where it needs to be constantly accurate. The user has to trust the outcome of their operations in the system. Having said this, it does not mean that the output has to be in synchrony. Things can eventually be consistent and accurate, just as long as the user is well informed. By allowing eventual consistency, one opens up a lot of benefits about how we build our software and you have a great opportunity to improve the user experience of the software you are building, which should be at the very forefront of your thinking when making software.

Eventual consistency basically means that the user performs an action and, asynchronously, it will be dealt with by the system and also eventually be performed. When it's actually performed, you could notify the user. If it fails, let the client know so that it can perform any compensating action or present something to the user. This is becoming a very common approach. It does impose a few new things to think about. We seldom build software that targets us as developers but has other users in mind when building it. This is the reason we go to work and build software for users. The user experience should, therefore, be the most important aspect and should always be the driving force and the main motive to apply a new technique. Of course, there are other aspects to decision making (such as budget) as this gives us business value, and so on. These are also the vital parts of the decision-making, but make sure that you never lose focus on the user.

How can we complete the circle and improve the model and take what we've learned and mix in a bit of real-time thinking? Instead of thinking that we need a response right away and pretty much locking up the user interface, we can send off the request for what we want and not wait for it at all. So, let the user carry on and then let the server tell us the result when it is ready. However, hang on, I mentioned accuracy; doesn't this mean that we would be sitting with a client in the wrong state? There are ways to deal with this in a user-friendly fashion. They are as follows:

- For simple things, you could assume that the server will perform the action and just perform the same on the client. This will give instant feedback to the user and the user can then carry on. If, for some reason, the action didn't succeed on the server, the server can, at a later stage, send the error related to the action that was performed and the client can perform a compensating action. Undoing this and notifying the user that it couldn't be performed is an example. An error should only be considered an edge case, so instead of modeling everything around the error, model the happy path and deal with the error on its own.

- Another approach would be to lock the particular element that was changed in the client but not the entire user interface, just the part that was modified or created. When the action succeeds and the server tells you, you can easily mark the element(s) as succeeded and apply the result from the server. Both of these techniques are valid and I would argue that you should apply both, depending on the circumstances.

SignalR

What does this all mean and how does SignalR fit into all this?

A regular vanilla web application without even being AJAX-enabled will do a full round-trip from the client to server for the entire page and all its parts when something is performed. This puts a strain on the server to serve the content and maybe even having to perform rendering on the server before returning the request. However, it also puts a strain on the bandwidth, having to return all the content all the time. AJAX-enabled web apps made this a lot better by typically not posting a full page back all the time. Today, with **Single Page Applications (SPA)**, we never do a full-page rendering or reloading and often not even rely on the server rendering anything. Instead, it just sits there serving static content in the form of HTML, CSS, and JavaScript files and then provides an API that can be consumed by the client.

SignalR goes a step further by representing an abstraction that gives you a persistent connection between the server and the client. You can send anything to the server and the server can at any time send anything back to the client, breaking the request/response pattern completely. We lose the overhead of the regular request or response pattern of the Web for every little thing that we need to do. From a resource perspective, you will end up needing less from both your server and your client. For instance, web requests are returned back to the request pool of ASP.NET as soon as possible and reduce the memory and CPU usage on the server.

By default, SignalR will choose the best way to accomplish this based on the capabilities of the client and the server combined. Ranging from WebSockets to Server Sent Events to Long Polling Requests, it promises to be able to connect a client and a server. If a connection is broken, SignalR will try to reestablish it from the client immediately.

Although SignalR uses long polling, the response going back from the server to a client is vastly improved rather than having to do a pull on an interval, which was the approach done for AJAX-enabled applications before.

You can force SignalR to choose a specific technique as long as you have requirements that limit what is allowed. However, when left as default, it will negotiate what is the best fit.

Terminology

As in any industry, we have a language that we use and it is not always ubiquitous. We might be saying the same thing but the meaning might vary. Throughout the book, you'll find terms being used in order for you to understand what is being referred to; I'll summarize what hides behind these terms mean.

Messaging

A message in computer software refers to a unit of communication that contains information that the source wants to communicate to the outside world, either to specific recipients or as a broadcast to all recipients connected now or in the future. The message itself is nothing, but a container holding information to identify the type of the message and the data associated with it. Messaging is used in a variety of ways. One way is either through the Win16/32 APIs with WM_* messages being sent for any user input or changes occurring in the UI. Another is things affecting the application to XML messages used to integrate systems. It could also be typed messages inside the software, modeled directly as a type. It comes in various forms, but the general purpose is to be able to do it in a decoupled manner that tells other parts that something has happened. The message and its identifier with its payload becomes the contract in which the decoupled systems know about. The two systems would not know about each other.

Publish/subscribe

With your message in place, you want to typically send it. Publish/subscribe, or, as it is known in shorthand "PubSub", is often what you're looking for. The message can be broadcasted and any part of your system can subscribe to the message by type and react to it. This decouples the components in your system by leaving a message for them, and they are unaware that they are direct to each other. This is achieved by having a message box sitting in the middle that all systems know about, which could be a local or global message box, depending on how your model thinks. The message box will then be given message calls, or will activate subscriptions, which are often specific to a message type or identifier.

Over the years, we've had all kinds of message boxes. In Windows, we have something called a message queue, which basically also acts as a message box. In addition, there are things such as service buses that pretty much do the same thing at the core as well. The notion of having something published and something else subscribed is not new.

The message box can be made smarter, which, for instance, could be by persisting all messages going through so that any future subscribers can be told what happened in the past. This is well presented by the following diagram:

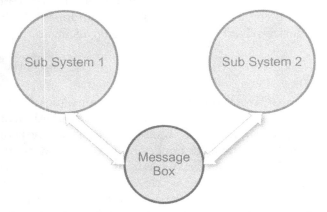

A representation of how the subsystems have a direct relationship with a message box, enabling the two systems to be decoupled from each other

Decoupling

There are quite a few paradigms in the art of programming and it all boils down to what is right for you. It's hard to argue what is right or wrong because the success of any paradigm is really hard to measure. Some people like a procedural approach to things where you can read end-to-end how a system is put together, which often leads to a much coupled solution. Solutions are things put together in a sequence and the elements can know about each other. The complete opposite approach would be to completely decouple things and break each problem into its own isolated unit with each unit not knowing about the other. This approach breaks everything down into more manageable units and helps keep complexity down. It really helps in the long term velocity of development and also how you can grow the functionality. In fact, it also helps with taking things out if one discovers one has features that aren't being used. By decoupling software and putting things in isolation and even sprinkle some **SOLID** on top of this (which is known as a collection of principles; this being the Single Responsibility Principle, Open/Closed Principle, Liskov Substitution Principle, Interface Segregation Principle, and Dependency Inversion Principle).

[You can find more information about this at
http://www.objectmentor.com/resources/
articles/Principles_and_Patterns.pdf.]

By applying these practices with decoupling in mind, we can:

- Make it easier to scale up your team with more developers; things will be separated out and responsibilities within the team can be done so as well.

- Make more maintainable solutions.

- Take resource hungry parts of your system and put them on separate servers; something that is harder to accomplish if it all is coupled together.

- Gain more flexibility by focusing more on each individual parts and then compose it back together any way you like.

- Make it easier to identify bottlenecks in isolation.

- Have less chance of breaking other parts of the system when fixing or expanding your code.

- Gain higher development pace.

- This might be a bold claim, but you could encounter fewer bugs! Or at least, they would be more maintainable bugs that sit inside isolated and focused code, making it easier to identity and safer to fix.

The ability to publish messages rather than calling concrete implementations becomes vital. These become the contracts within your system.

This book will constantly remind you of one thing: users are a big part in making this decision. Making your system flexible and more maintainable is of interest to your users. The turnaround time to fix bugs along with delivering new features is very much in their interest. One of the things I see a lot in projects is that we tend to try to define everything way too early and often upfront of development, taking an end-to-end design approach. This often leads to overthinking and often coupling, making it harder to change later on when we know more. By making exactly what is asked for and not trying to be too creative and add things that could be nice to have, and then really thinking of small problems and rather compose it back together, the chance of success is bigger and also easier to maintain and change. Having said this, decoupling is, ironically enough, tightly coupled with the SOLID principles along with other principles to really accomplish this. For instance, take the S in SOLID. This represents the **Single Responsibility Principle**; it governs that a single unit should not do more than one thing. A unit can go all the way down to a method. Breaking up things into more tangible units, rather than huge unreadable units, makes your code more flexible and more readable.

 Decoupling will play a vital role in the remainder of the book.

Patterns

Techniques that repeat can be classified as patterns; you probably already have a bunch of patterns in your own code that you might classify even as your own patterns. Some of these become popular outside the realms of one developer's head and are promoted beyond just this one guy. A pattern is a well-understood solution to a particular problem. They are identified rather than *created*. That is, they emerge and are abstracted from solutions to real-world problems rather than being imposed on a problem from the outside. It's also a common vocabulary that allows developers to communicate more efficiently.

A popular book that aims to gather some of these patterns is *Design Patterns: Elements of Reusable Object-Oriented Software* by *Erich Gamma, Richard Helm, Ralph Johnson,* and *John Vlissides, Addison-Wesley Professional.*

You can find a copy at http://www.amazon.com/Design-Patterns-Elements-Reusable-Object-Oriented/dp/0201633612.

We will be using different patterns throughout this book, so it's important to understand what they are, the reasons behind them, and how they are applied successfully. The following sections will give you a short summary of the patterns being referred to and used.

Model View Controller

Interestingly enough, most of the patterns we have started applying have been around for quite a while. The **Model View Controller** (**MVC**) pattern is a great example of this.

MVC was first introduced by a fellow Norwegian national called Dr. Trygve Reenskaug in 1973 in a paper called Administrative Control in the Shipyard (http://martinfowler.com/eaaDev/uiArchs.html). Since then, it has been applied successfully in a variety of frameworks and platforms. With the introduction of Ruby on Rails in 2005, I would argue the focus on MVC really started to get traction in the modern web development sphere. When Microsoft published ASP.NET MVC at the end of 2007, they helped gain focus in the .NET community as well.

The purpose of MVC is to decouple the elements in the frontend and create a better isolated focus on these different concerns. Basically, what one has is a controller that governs the actions that are allowed to be performed for a particular feature of your application. The actions can return a result in the form of either data or concrete new views to navigate to. The controller is responsible for holding and providing any state to the views through the actions it exposes. By state, we often think of the model and often the data comes from a database, either directly exposed or adapted into a view-specific model that suits the view better than the raw data from the database. The relationship between model, controller, view, and the user is well summarized in the following diagram:

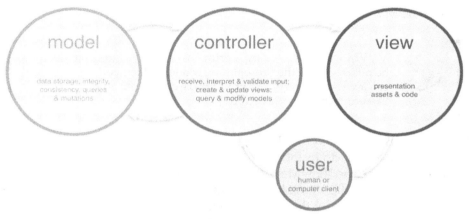

A representation of how the artifacts make up MVC (don't forget there is a user that will interact with all of these artifacts)

With this approach, you separate out the presentation aspect of the business logic into the controller. The controller then has a relationship with other subsystems that knows the other aspects of the business logic in a better manner, allowing the controller to only focus on the logic that is specific to the presentation and not on any concrete business logic but more on the presentation aspect of any business logic. This decouples it from the underlying subsystem and thus more specialized. The view now has to concern itself with only view-related things, which are typically HTML and CSS for web applications. The model, either a concrete model from the database or adapted for the view, is fetched from whatever data source you have.

Model View ViewModel

Extending on the promise of decoupling in the frontend, we get something called **Model View ViewModel** (short for **MVVM**).

 For more information, visit http://www.codeproject.com/ Articles/100175/Model-View-ViewModel-MVVM-Explained.

This is a design pattern for the frontend based largely on MVC, but it takes it a bit further in terms of decoupling. From this, Microsoft created a specialization that happened to be MVVM.

 MVVM was presented by Martin Fowler in 2004 to what he referred to as the Presentation Model (which you can access at http://martinfowler.com/eaaDev/ PresentationModel.html).

The ViewModel is a key player in this that holds the state and behavior needed for your feature to be able to do its job, without it knowing about the view. The view will then be observing the ViewModel for any changes it might get and utilize any behaviors it exposes. In the ViewModel, we keep the state, and as with MVC, the state is in the form of a model that could be a direct model coming from your data source or an adapted model more fine-tuned for the purpose of the frontend.

The additional decoupling, which this model represents, lies within the fact that the ViewModel has no clue to any view, and in fact should be blissfully unaware that it is being used in a view. This makes the code even more focused and it opens an opportunity of being able to swap out the view at any given time or even reuse the same ViewModel with its logic and state for second view.

The relationship between the **model**, **view**, **viewmodel**, and the **user** is summarized in the following diagram:

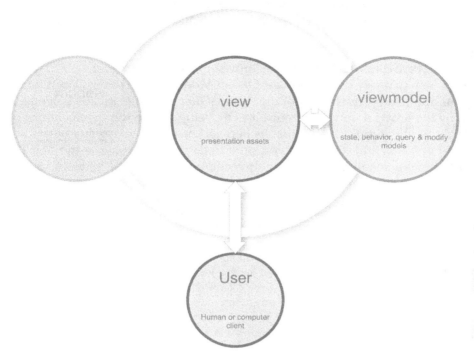

The artefacts that make up MVVM. As a reminder, don't forget that the user interacts with these artifacts through the view.

Libraries and frameworks

We will not be doing much from scratch in this book as it does not serve our purpose. Instead, we will be relying on third-party libraries and frameworks to do things for us that don't have anything to do with the particular thing we will perform. The range of libraries will be big and some of these represent architectural patterns and decisions sitting behind them. Some of these are in direct conflict with each other and for consistency in your code base, you should pick one over the other and stick to it. The chapters in this book will make it clear what I consider as conflict and why and what libraries are right for you, whereas your architecture is something you will have to decide for yourself. This book will just show a few of the possibilities.

jQuery

Browsing the Web for JavaScript-related topics often yields results with jQuery mentioned in the subject or in the article itself. At one point, I was almost convinced that JavaScript started with $, followed by a dot, and then a function to perform. It turns out that this is not true. jQuery just happens to be one of the most popular libraries out there when performing web development. It puts in place abstractions for parts that are different between the browsers, but most importantly, it gives you a powerful way to query the **Document Object Model (DOM)** as well as modify pick it as your application runs. A lot of the things jQuery has historically solved are now solved by the browser vendors themselves by being true to the specifications of the standards, along with the standards. Its demand has been decreasing over the years, but you will find it useful if you need to target all browsers and not just the modern ones. Personally, I would highly recommend not using jQuery as it will most likely lead you down the path of breaking the SOLID principles and mixing up your concerns.

SignalR has a dependency on jQuery directly, meaning that all the web projects in this book will have jQuery in them as a result. The part of jQuery being used is the communication stack (anything else is not used). There are projects out there that aim towards trimming jQuery. You might find something that only holds the communication part of jQuery, reducing the payload dramatically, since I do not recommend using jQuery for DOM manipulation.

ASP.NET MVC 5

Microsoft's web story consists of two major and different stories at the root level. One of these is the story related to web forms that came with the first version of the .NET Framework back in 2002. Since then, it has been iteratively developed and improved with each new version of the framework. The other is the MVC story, which was started in 2007 with a version 1 release in 2009 that represents something very different and built from the ground up from different concepts than found in the web forms story. In 2014, we saw the release of version 5 with quite a few new ideas, making it even simpler to do the type of decoupling one aims for and also making it easier to bring in things (such as SignalR). We will use ASP.NET MVC for the first samples, not taking full advantage of its potential, but enough to be able to show the integration with SignalR and how you can benefit from it.

AngularJS

It seems that over the last couple of years, you can pretty much take any noun or verb and throw a JS behind it, Google it, and you will find a framework at the other end of it. All these frameworks often play as a part of the puzzle. Google introduced AngularJS a couple of years ago to cover more than just a little part of the puzzle, but it rather provides a broader perspective on client-side development on the Web. AngularJS consists of a core and modules that cover different aspects. With AngularJS, you get the opportunity to separate your code into smaller parts, promoting separation and lending itself to MVC and to a certain extent MVVM. Throughout this book, we will be using Angular for the web solution.

Twitter Bootstrap

In the interest of saving time and focusing more on code, we will "outsource" the design in this book and layout to Twitter Bootstrap (which you can access at `http://getbootstrap.com`). Bootstrap defines a grid system that governs all layouts and it also has well-defined CSS to make things look good. It comes with a predefined theme that looks great, and there are other themes out there if you want to change the themes.

Tools

As with any craft, we need tools to build anything. Here is a summary of some of the tools we will be using to create our applications.

Visual Studio 2013

In this book, you will find that Visual Studio 2013 Professional is used. For the iOS content, we will be using Visual Studio—although it is in conjunction with Xamarin and Apple's Xcode.

 You can use the community edition of Visual Studio 2013 if you don't have a license to Visual Studio 2013 professional or higher. It can be downloaded from `http://www.visualstudio.com/`.

NuGet

All third-party dependencies and all the libraries mentioned in this chapter, for instance, will be pulled in using NuGet.

 In the interest of saving space in the book, the description of how to use NuGet sits here and only here. The other chapters will refer back to this recipe.

If you need to install NuGet first, visit `http://www.nuget.org` to download and install it. Once this is done, you can use NuGet by following these steps:

1. To add a reference to a project, we start by right-clicking on **References** of your project and selecting **Manage NuGet Packages...**, as shown here:

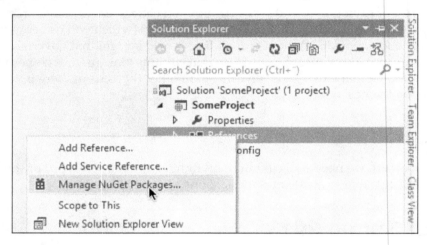

2. Next, select **Online** and enter the name of the package that you want to add a reference to in the search box. When you have found the proper package, click on the **Install** button, as shown in the following screenshot:

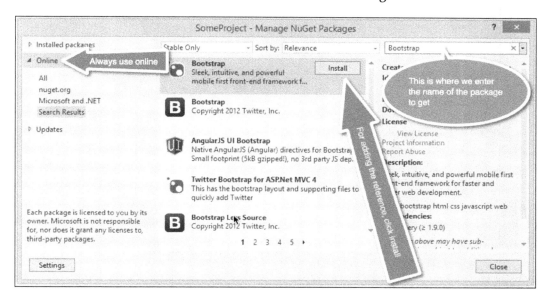

 In some cases, we will need a specific version of a file. This is not something we can do through the UI, and we will need the Package Manager Console. To specify a specific version of a package, if needed, the syntax of the command in the Package Manager Console is as follows:

```
install-package <package-name> -version <package-version>
```

3. Following this, go to **TOOLS** and then **NuGet Package Manager**. Click on **Package Manager Console**, as shown here:

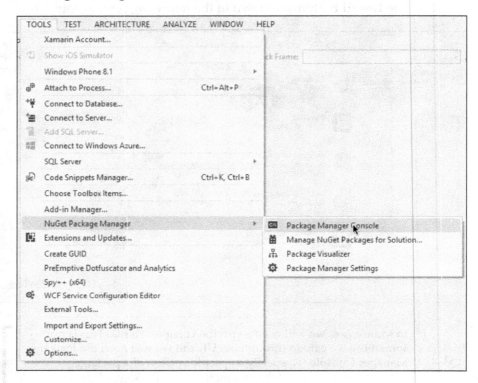

4. You then need to go to the **Package Manager Console** window that appears and you need to make sure that the project that will have the reference is selected:

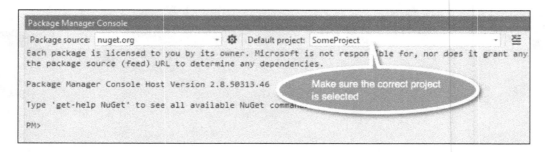

By now, you should be familiar with how you can add NuGet packages to reference third-party dependencies, which will be used throughout the book.

Summary

You now have a backdrop of knowledge, if you didn't already know it all. We explained the terminology in this chapter so that the terms will be clear to you throughout. It's now time to get concrete and actually start applying what we've discussed. Although this chapter mentions quite a few concepts and they might be new to you, don't worry as we'll revisit them throughout the book and gain more knowledge about them as we go along. The next chapter will start out with a simple sample, showing the very basics of SignalR so that you get the feeling of what it is and how its APIs are. It will also establish the basics of the project that we will be working on throughout this book, with ASP.NET and AngularJS throwing bootstrap into the mix as well.

2
Persistent Connections

For years in network programming, we have been using sockets and communicating with these. Although we now have sockets on the Web as well, we are not guaranteed that we will have it in all environments. We, therefore, need an abstraction that helps us out with this and picks the right transport mechanism for us. In comes persistent connections. This chapter will cover the basics of getting a client connected to the server and how the messaging works.

In this chapter, the following topics will be covered:

- Getting started with single-page applications
- Getting started with AngularJS
- Setting up a web application with SignalR
- Exposing a persistent connection on the server
- Consuming the connection in a JavaScript client

At this stage, the developer should be having the beginning of a single-page web application connected to a server.

Persistent connections – what are they?

At the core of SignalR sits the abstraction that represents an actual connection. This is the lowest level of the abstraction and it is the thing that deals with connecting the client to the server and abstracting away the negotiation for protocol, and in general all communication. One could look at this as what is known as the socket connection in regular TCP/IP development. Although it is a bit easier, since you're not having to deal with byte buffers, but strings instead.

Where are we going?

The remainder of this book will try to keep to the narrow path of developing iteratively on the same application; a chat application with a web client, a .NET WPF client, and a Xamarin-based mobile client, all working with the same server. We will also go into how to self-host SignalR in your own app for any clients to connect to, without having to have a web server installed and configured.

Getting the project ready

Our project will have a server component to it; the server component will also be hosting the web client that we will be using.

1. Start by creating a new project in Visual Studio:

2. Select the regular empty **ASP.NET Web Application** project template
    situated under **Visual C# | Web**. Give it a name: `SignalRChat`. Make sure
    Add Application Insights to Project is unchecked. Then, click on **OK**:

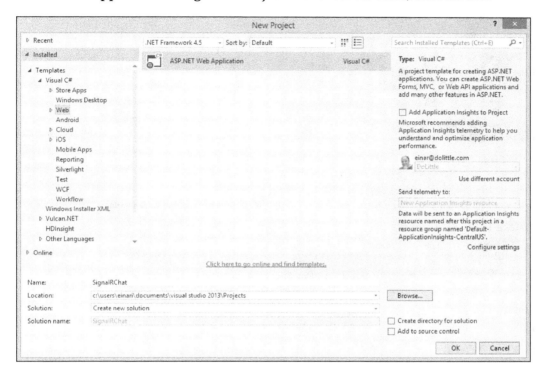

3. Select the **Empty** template and make sure **Host in the cloud** is left unchecked. Then, click on **OK**:

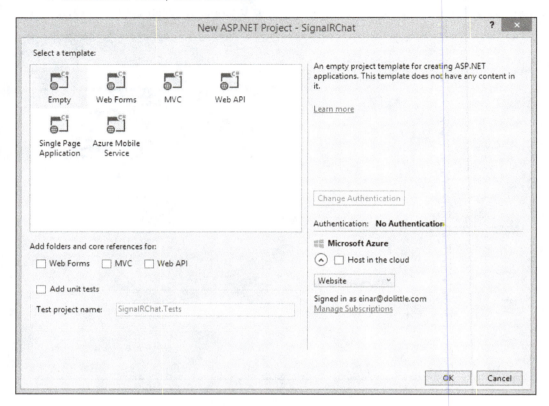

Setting up the packages

Now, we will need some packages to get things started. This process is described in detail in *Chapter 1, The Primer*. Let's start off with adding SignalR, which is our primary framework that we will be working with to move on. We will be pulling this using NuGet, as described in *Chapter 1, The Primer*; right-click on **References** in **Solution Explorer** and select **Manage NuGet Packages**, and type `Microsoft.AspNet.SignalR` in the Search panel. Select this and click on **Install**. For our web project, we will need some more things. Firstly, we will need a package called AngularJS; repeat the NuGet process using AngularJS in the Search panel. The final package we will need for now is Bootstrap; repeat the NuGet process again and this time enter Bootstrap in the Search panel.

The single page application

In modern web development, you're bound to come across the concept of a single-page application, which is often just referred to as SPA. The concept behind this is very simple; it's not about navigating the entire page away once we've hit a site or application. The first page that we hit will then be responsible for composing everything after that, based on what the user does. This often results in more work for the client than the server, which is really a good thing. It means better separation of concerns, letting the client do what they are good at and likewise for the server. There are quite a few frameworks out there promoting this way of working, some more complete than others. One of the more popular ones these days is something that came out of Google called **AngularJS**. It is one of the complete frameworks, providing pretty much all the client aspects you can think of. It is an open source framework and is being developed rapidly. At the time of writing this book, the latest version is 1.3.15, and the development of version 2 is well on its way with a few changes. In an SPA, one needs an entry point for the application, the page that holds it all:

1. Let's add the page that we will be hitting for our first request, our index. Right-click on the project in **Solution Explorer** and select **Add | New Item**. Navigate to **Web** in the template tree to the left and select **HTML Page**. Give the file a name index.html:

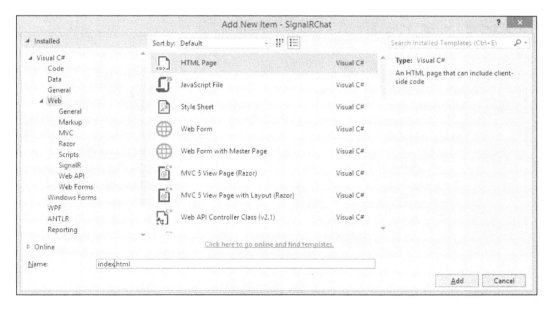

2. Within the HEAD tag on the top of the newly created file, we will need to add references to Bootstrap. Add the following two references:

```
<link href="Content/bootstrap.min.css" rel="stylesheet" />
<link href="Content/bootstrap-theme.min.css" rel="stylesheet" />
```

3. On the top of the page, we want to have a navigation bar. For now, there won't be any things to navigate to, but we want it there from the start. Within the BODY tag, add the following:

```
<nav class="navbar navbar-inverse">
    <div class="container-fluid">
        <div class="navbar-header">
            <span class="navbar-brand">SignalR Chat</span>
        </div>
    </div>
</nav>
```

4. At the bottom of the BODY tag, before it ends, we want to keep our script references:

```
<script src="Scripts/jquery-1.9.1.min.js" type="text/
javascript"></script>
<script src="Scripts/bootstrap.min.js" type="text/javascript"></
script>
<script src="Scripts/angular.js" type="text/javascript"></script>
<script src="Scripts/jquery.signalR-2.2.0.min.js"></script>
```

Keeping the script references at the bottom of the page while keeping the stylesheet references in the head ensures that the user gets something on the screen as fast as possible. Script downloads actually block the rendering process, so keeping these at the bottom will make sure rendering starts as soon as possible. Stylesheets providing the look alongside the HTML inside the BODY will render it for the user before it starts pulling down scripts.

It is worth mentioning here that the version numbers in the preceding code snippet may be different from yours; look inside the Scripts folder to make sure you're referencing the right versions.

5. Running the application by pressing *CTRL + F5* (**Debug | Start Without Debugging**) should yield the following output:

6. We will need to configure AngularJS. To do that, we want to have our own JavaScript file that configures our application with AngularJS. Add a JavaScript file by right-clicking on the project and select **Add | New Item**. Select **JavaScript File** and give it a name `config.js`.

7. We want to have a stricter interpretation of the JavaScript, so add the following line on top of the new file:

```
"use strict";
```

The `"use strict"` directive tells the JavaScript engine to execute in `"strict mode"`. With this, you will get errors for things that can potentially be creating problems in your code. An example of this would be global variables. This is considered pollution of the global scope and will therefore be considered as a potential problem in strict mode.

8. Let's add a scope where we can configure AngularJS and more:

```
(function (global) {
})(window);
```

A scope is a self-executing function that gives you, among other things, a simple way to keep local variables without polluting the global scope. We pass the window instance as a parameter to the inner function, which becomes known as global within that function scope. This ensures that even if the window changed the reference outside our scope, we won't be affected.

9. Within the function, we will need to configure our main AngularJS module. Put the following code within the inner function:

```
var application = angular.module("SignalRChat");

application.config(["$provide",
    function ($provide) {
    }
]);

global.$application = application;
```

> Firstly, the module definition is given a name SignalRChat. Secondly, we give it an array of modules we rely on. In our case, we will only need the core AngularJS module for now: ng.
>
> The application variable is put into a global scope (window) for accessibility later. In our particular case, we will have only one module. However, in AngularJS, you could potentially have multiple. This is a question of how you structure your application.

10. Let's go back to the index.html file and hook up AngularJS and the config file that we've just added. We want to use the application module that we just registered by making the HTML tag look as follows:

```
<html ng-app="SignalRChat">
```

11. The next thing we want to do is add a script reference to the config.js file; add the following script tag after all the other tags:

```
<script src="config.js" type="text/javascript"></script>
```

The "code-behind"

AngularJS is a MVW framework; W stands for whatever. Although being this flexible and non opinionated, it does have the concept of a controller. A controller is responsible for managing the state and behavior exposed to the view. It is typically the place that coordinates the interaction with other systems, such as services, that communicate with the server by getting data and pushing actions back to the server.

With AngularJS, we get something called an **Inversion of Control (IoC)** container. This is a system that is responsible for the life cycle of objects and assumes the **Dependency Inversion Principle**. This principle states that you are not responsible for your dependencies, instead you specify your dependencies and the IOC container will make sure to create them and provide them to your system. This will become very clear when we define our controller.

1. Let's add a new JavaScript file in the root of the project called `index.js`. Right-click on the project and select **Add | New Item**. Select **JavaScript File** and give it a name `index.js`.

2. Put the following code into the newly created file:

```
"use strict";
$application.controller("index", ["$scope", function ($scope) {
}]);
```

 Notice the usage of the `$application` instance that we set up during our configuration. This is why we made this global.

3. Now, we will associate an element in the HTML with the controller. Open up the `index.html` file and make the `BODY` tag look as follows:

```
<body ng-controller="index">
```

4. The last thing we will need for the controller to actually work is to have the `index.js` file loaded. Add the following `script` tag after the other `script` tags:

```
<script src="index.js" type="text/javascript"></script>
```

The first parameter in the controller function is the name of the controller; we are consistent with naming the controller and the file the same, except losing the file extension for the name of the controller. The second parameter of a controller definition is an array holding all the dependencies and, as the last element of the array, the function that defines the controller. The parameters are specified as string literals; these strings are the names that identify the dependencies and are typically what they are registered with in the IOC container. In the function that represents the controller, the same dependencies are again specified in the same order as they appear in the array of strings before.

AngularJS supports specifying the dependencies by its parameter name in the function that represents the controller only, leaving the array definition without any string literals at all. However, if you want to typically minimize or uglify your JavaScript, the names of the parameters would be changed and they would not match what they are defined as.

Getting started with the server-side

We will need some C# code to initialize the server side of things.

SignalR is configured through something called **Open Web Interface for .NET (OWIN)**. There are other, more traditional ways of doing this, but this is the preferred way and also conceptually how things are evolving in the ASP.NET space. We will be using it throughout the book in different forms.

 Its goal is to define a standard interface between .NET web servers and web applications. Read more at http://owin.org.

1. Let's add a class called `Startup` to the project. Right-click on the project and select **Add | Class**. Give the file a name `Startup.cs`.

2. Replace all the using statements with the following:
   ```
   using Microsoft.Owin;
   using Owin;
   ```

3. Inside the `Startup` class, we will a `Configuration` method. Make the class look as follows:
   ```
   public class Startup
   {
       public void Configuration(IAppBuilder app)
       {
       }
   }
   ```

4. As you can see, the class is not inheriting anything or implementing an interface. The signature is a convention defined. However, in order for OWIN to pick up this, we must tell OWIN where to look. Let's add an attribute between the `using` statements and the `namespace` statement:

   ```
   [assembly: OwinStartup(typeof(SignalRChat.Startup))]
   ```

There is another way of telling OWIN where to look: you can do this in `Web.config`:

```
<appSettings>
  <add key="owin:appStartup" value="SignalRChat.
Startup" />
</appSettings>
```

Connecting the dots

SignalR has at its core an abstraction called `PersistentConnection`. This is the building block that everything else builds upon. This chapter will show you how we can start using this building block and achieve results very fast. First, we will need a type representing our connection:

1. Add a class called `ChatConnection.cs` to the root of the project.

2. Add the following using statements:

```
using System.Threading.Tasks;
using Microsoft.AspNet.SignalR;
```

3. Make the class inherit from `PersistentConnection`:

```
public class ChatConnection : PersistentConnection
{
}
```

4. In order for us to handle messages being sent from the client, we need to override a method called `OnReceived`. We will take whatever data we get into that method and broadcast it to all the connected clients. Put the following method in the `ChatConnection` class:

```
protected override Task OnReceived(IRequest request, string
connectionId, string data)
{
    return Connection.Broadcast(data);
}
```

With `Broadcast`, you will be sending the data to all connected clients, including the one who was sending. You can use one of the method overloads if you want to filter connections on the broadcast.

5. Now, we will have to expose the connection we just created so that it can be consumed by any connecting clients . Open up the `Startup.cs` file. In the `Configuration` method, add the following line:

```
app.MapConnection<ChatConnection>("/chat");
```

6. With the server code in place, we need to move back to the client and hook up the connection. Open up the `config.js` file and put the following code into the configuration function that has `$provide` as an argument:

```
var chatConnection = $.connection("/chat");

chatConnection.start().done(function () {
    console.log("Started");
});

$provide.constant("chat", chatConnection);
```

SignalR is built on top of jQuery, and we find all functionalities for SignalR inside the $ - jQuery object. The `connection` function gets a `connection` object for the connection URL specified.

The `start()` function returns what is known as a promise, which is an object exposing a function called `done()`. This takes a function that gets called when we are connected. When one starts a connection, SignalR starts the negotiation with the server to find the most optimal connection type that works best with the client and the server capabilities.

As mentioned before, AngularJS has an IOC container that controls objects and the life cycle. The `$provide` dependency that we've taken into the configuration function, exposes the functionality that we need to configure these dependencies. There are different ways to register; in our case, we specify it as a constant. The constant, we specify, named `chat` points to `chatConnection` and will always just be that instance. Another option is to use factory that we will revisit later.

With the server up and running and the basic client code for connecting, we can run the application again (*CTRL + F5* or **Debug | Run Without Debugger**). All the modern browsers have a developer tool built into it; this is typically accessible by hitting the *F12* key. With the code running, you should now see a **Started** message in the console of the developer tool.

Thus, so far, you've actually created a client that connects to a server and keeps that connection open throughout the life cycle of the application. This was done with little effort, I might add, as well.

Making the UI light up

Now, we're ready to actually make a UI and hook it up to the code that connects to the server.

In AngularJS, there is something called as scope that we need to be aware of. You may have noticed on the controller setup that there was a dependency going into the controller called $scope. This is something that AngularJS automatically resolves with a factory it has built in. A scope is basically a place where we can put variables that we want to use for binding in the view and also expose the behavior that we want to use in the view. The scope typically inherits a parent scope, making the parent's state and behavior accessible for use. I would, however, be careful about doing so, as this opens up new and interesting ways to couple your code together, making it harder to change. Typically, AngularJS introduces a new level in the hierarchy for each controller within the DOM. We're now going to add the actual chat window and input field for chatting:

1. Open up the index.html file and add the following HTML inside the BODY tag after the navigation bar and before the script tags:

```
<div class="container">
    <div class="row">
        <div class="col-md-4">
            <textarea id="chatWindow" style="width:400px;
height:200px;" ng-model="messages"></textarea>

            <div class="form-inline">
                <div class="form-group">
                    <label for="messageTextBox" class="control-
label">Message</label>
                    <div class="input-group">
                        <input type="text" class="form-control"
id="messageTextBox" placeholder="Message" ng-model="message">
                    </div>
                    <button type="submit" class="btn btn-primary"
ng-click="click()">Send</button>
                </div>
            </div>
        </div>
    </div>
</div>
```

Note that, on the textarea tag, we're using an attribute called ng-model. This is an AngularJS directive, making the textarea bind its value attribute, to a variable in the scope. You'll notice that it is being used for the input tag as well. A second directive is also being used: ng-click. This is used to specify as to what to do when an element, typically a button, is clicked. In our code, we have specified it to call a function called click.

2. Open up the index.js file. Now, we want to change the signature of the controller to take the chat connection as a parameter. Make the controller definition look as follows:

```
$application.controller("index", ["$scope", "chat", function
($scope, chat) {
```

3. Since we have specified the view to bind to things in the scope, we need to get these things in place. Within the controller function, add the following code:

```
$scope.messages = "Connected";

$scope.click = function () {
    chat.send($scope.message);
};
```

 Note that chat.send() takes the message variable from the scope and sends it to the chat connection.

4. The last thing we will need is a function that receives any messages from the chat and puts it into the messages variable. Add the following after the click handler:

```
chat.received(function (data) {
    $scope.$apply(function () {
        $scope.messages = $scope.messages + "\n" + data;
    });
});
```

On any connection in the client, we have a received function that makes it possible for us to register callbacks that get called when data is received. The signature takes the actual data as a parameter. The call to $apply is needed in order to tell AngularJS that the scope variable is changing, so it can update its bindings.

Our basic chat application should now be up and running. Run a couple of browsers side by side, and start typing messages and send them. This should be giving you something as follows:

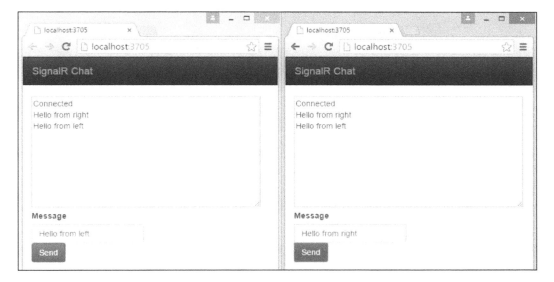

Summary

We've seen how easy it is to get started with SignalR and set up a persistent connection. With AngularJS, we've also started seeing how to structure a single-page application. With the little effort put in this chapter, we are already sending a message for our chat application across browsers.

Moving forward from this point, we will be looking at this with a different abstraction, hubs in SignalR, providing a way to expose functionality on the server more naturally.

3
Hubs

With persistent connections, we have to manage everything going back and forth with the server. The only thing abstracted away is the transport. Typically, in applications, you are looking at calling well-defined resources on the server and would probably want to deal with those rather than the raw power of persistent connections. This chapter will cover how you connect a client with a server in a very different way, making it seem like you can call code directly on the client from the server and vice versa.

Topics covered in this chapter are as follows:

- Setting up a hub on the server
- Working with hubs
- Consuming a hub from a JavaScript client
- Improving the usage of a hub in an AngularJS application

At this stage, the developer should be able to use a hub, and our sample app will now be able to chat properly.

Moving up a level

While `PersistentConnection` seems very easy to work with, it is the lowest level of abstraction in SignalR. It does provide the perfect abstraction for keeping a connection open between a client and a server, but that's just about all it does provide. Working with different operations is not far from how you would deal with things in a regular socket connection, where you basically have to parse whatever is coming from a client and figure out which operation needs to be performed based on the input. SignalR provides a higher level of abstraction that removes this need and you can write your server-side code in a more intuitive manner. In SignalR, this higher level of abstraction is called a hub.

Basically, a hub represents an abstraction that allows you to write classes with methods that takes different parameters, as you would with any API in your application, and then makes it completely transparent on the client—at least for JavaScript. This resembles a concept called **Remote Procedure Call (RPC)**, with many incarnations of it out there.

For our chat application, at this stage, we basically just want to be able to send a message from a client to the server and have it send the message to all the other clients connected. To do this, we will now move away from the `PersistentConnection` and introduce a new class called `Hub` using the following steps:

1. First, start off by deleting the `ChatConnection` class from your web project.

2. Then, we want to add a hub implementation instead. Right-click on the **SignalRChat** project and select **Add | New Item**.

3. In the dialog box, choose **Class** and give it a name `Chat.cs`:

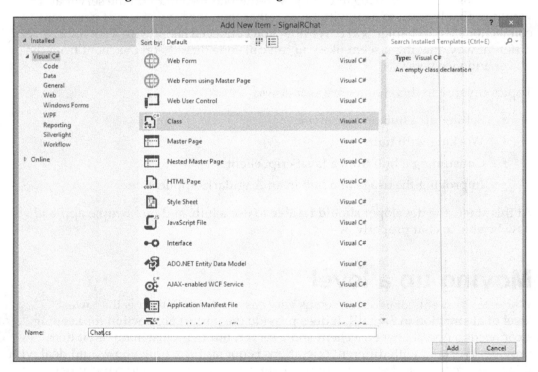

4. This is the class that will represent our `Hub`. Make it inherit from `Hub`:

```
public class Chat : Hub
```

5. Add the necessary import statement at the top of the file:

```
using Microsoft.AspNet.SignalR.Hubs;
```

6. In the class, we will add a simple method that will be the one that the clients will call to send a message. We call the method `Send` and take one parameter into it; a string that contains the message being sent by the client:

```
public void Send(string message)
{
}
```

7. From the base class of `Hub`, we get a few things that we can use. For now, we'll be using the `clients` property to broadcast to all other clients connected to the `Hub`. On the `clients` property, you'll find an `All` property, which is dynamic. On this, we can call anything and the client will just have to subscribe to the method we call, if the client is interested:

```
using Microsoft.AspNet.SignalR;

namespace SignalRChat
{
    public class Chat : Hub
    {
        public void Send(string message)
        {
            Clients.All.addMessage(message);
        }
    }
}
```

8. The next thing we need to do is to go into the `Startup.cs` file and make some changes. Firstly, we remove the `.MapSignalR<ChatConnection>(...)` line and replace it with a `.MapSignalR()` call that does not specify a connection as a parameter. This will map up all hubs in your application automatically with a default path for your hubs that maps to `/signalr/<name of hub>`: so more concretely the path will be: `http://<your-site>:port/signalr/<name of hub>`. We're going with the defaults for now. It should cover the needs on the server-side code. Your `Startup` class should look as follows:

```
using Microsoft.Owin;
using Owin;
```

```
[assembly: OwinStartup(typeof(SignalRChat.Startup))]

namespace SignalRChat
{
    public class Startup
    {
        public void Configuration(IAppBuilder app)
        {
            app.MapSignalR();
        }
    }
}
```

It is possible to change the name of the Hub to not be the same as the class name. An attribute called HubName() can be placed in front of the class to give it a new name. The attribute takes one parameter: the name you want for your Hub. Similarly, for methods inside your Hub, you can use an attribute called HubMethodName() to give the method a different name.

The client

Now that we have the server setup done, we're ready to move on to the client. Out of the box, SignalR comes with very simple ways of consuming any hubs that are created. We're not going to use these methods since we have the power of AngularJS in our solution; we want to do things in conjunction with how AngularJS does things.

Decoupling it all

AngularJS talks about **Model View Whatever (MVW)**. There are a few frontend patterns that resemble each other and they share a common goal: decoupling and making the different concerns in the frontend more clear. The alternative to thinking in these manners is typically a model where the different concerns are all mixed together and coupled in a way that makes it harder to change. By thinking about the different concerns and separating these out, you have identified the responsibility and can make the different parts more specialized and focused. Although AngularJS lends itself, in terminology, more towards **Model View Controller** (MVC), over the years I've grown fond of the pattern called **Model View ViewModel** (MVVM), and even though I'm doing AngularJS from time to time, I still like to think in this manner.

MVVM is a pattern for client development that became very popular in the XAML stack, enabled by Microsoft based on Martin Fowlers presentation model (http://martinfowler.com/eaaDev/PresentationModel.html). Its principle is that you have a ViewModel that holds the state and exposes behavior that can be utilized from a view. The view observes any changes of the state the ViewModel exposes, making the ViewModel totally unaware that there is a view. The ViewModel is decoupled and can be put in isolation and is perfect for automated testing. As part of the state that the ViewModel typically holds is the model part, which is something it usually gets from the server, and a SignalR hub is the perfect transport to get this. In AngularJS, the controller in combination with the scope can be looked upon as representing a ViewModel. It boils down to recognizing the different concerns that make up the frontend and separating it all. This gives us the following diagram:

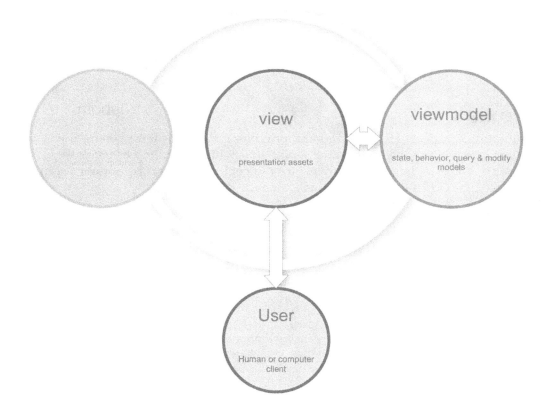

The Dependency Inversion Principle

Robert C. Martin coined the concept of SOLID in programming
(`http://butunclebob.com/ArticleS.UncleBob.PrinciplesOfOod`). These are a
set of principles that will help you create code that is more maintainable and easier
to understand. We will not go through all these principles as they are well defined
elsewhere, but it is important to understand the D in SOLID as it's widely used in
AngularJS. The concept of dependency inversion says that instead of a unit knowing
how to get its dependencies, it will be governed by something else. Dependencies are
traditionally also seen as contracts, and the system would only rely on the contract,
not on the concrete implementation. This is flipping the responsibility around
completely and saying that your system does not need to know about concrete
implementations, nor does it need to think about life cycle. With this, we get the
Inversion of Control (IoC) container.

We have already used and mentioned the IOC in *Chapter 2, Persistent Connections*.
During the setup of AngularJS in the config.js file, we saw the usage of `$provide`.
This represents the IOC.

Proxies

An important aspect of SignalR is that it provides a mechanism for generating
proxies representing the hubs on the server-side, which is written in a statically
compiled .NET language. The simplest way to get the proxies is by adding a script
reference that points to a route that will generate it at runtime.

1. JavaScript proxies become available from your hubs when they're mapped
    using `.MapSignalR()`; they are also subject to the same default URL, but will
    follow the configuration given to `.MapSignalR()`.We will need to include a
    script reference in the HTML right after the line that references the SignalR
    JavaScript file; we will add the following:

    ```
    <script src="/signalr/hubs" type="text/javascript"></script>
    ```

     This will include the generated proxies for our JavaScript client.
    What this means is that we get whatever is exposed on a Hub
    generated for us, and we can start using it straightaway.

2. The proxies in SignalR are built in a specific way with a particular behavior. In order for clients to be able to have their client functions called, the client functions have to be set before initializing the hub connection to the server. In a typical single page application, this is inconvenient as you only want the hub connection to be initialized once. We will work around this by mending the proxies a bit at runtime. Open the config.js file and put the following code after the (function (global) {, which is the start of the scope line:

```
function __nothing() { }

function setupAndRegisterProxies($provide) {

    for (var property in $.connection) {
        var value = $.connection[property];
        if (typeof value !== "undefined" && value !== null) {
            if (typeof value.hubName !== "undefined" && value !==
null) {
                var hubName = property;
                var proxy = $.connection.hub.
createHubProxy(hubName);


                proxy.client.__need_this_for_subscription__ = __
nothing;
                registerHubFactory($provide, hubName);
            }
        }
    }
}
```

By putting in need_this_for_subscription and pointing it to the __nothing function, we force SignalR to set up a subscription back to the server. This is something it won't do if there are no functions defined on the client object sitting inside the proxy.

3. At the end, it calls a function called `registerHubFactory()` that is missing at the moment. Before the code that you just put in, add the following:

```
function registerHubFactory($provide, hubName) {
    $provide.factory(hubName, function () {
        var proxy = $.connection.hub.createHubProxy(hubName);
        return proxy;
    });
}
```

The `$provide` object in AngularJS has different ways to register dependencies. As we saw in *Chapter 2, Persistent Connections,* we used the `.constant()` function to register. This gave us an object that only has one instance in the life cycle of the application, or the page, seeing it is a web application. With the `registerHubFactory()` function, we're registering a factory that will be responsible for resolving the hub dependency whenever it is needed. This factory is nothing but a function that gets called when something needs the dependency. In our case, we just forward the creation to SignalR itself.

4. Now, we want to change the configuration of the application object in `config.js`. Swap out the existing `.config()` call to look as follows:

```
application.config(["$provide",
    function ($provide) {
        setupAndRegisterProxies($provide);

        $.connection.hub.start().done(function () {
            console.log("Hub connection up and running");
        });
    }
]);
```

This will set up all the proxies properly and also make sure we have the hub connection started and running. We only need to connect once for a single-page application; SignalR will maintain the connection and make sure that we reconnect if it is broken. Surely, if you need to know when it is connected or disconnected, you can either expose the connection object itself as a dependency for AngularJS, or a wrapper object with the needed functionality. The latter will make sure you don't expose too much power throughout your application.

5. Now that we have all the configuration taken care of, we can start making use of the hub. The chat object has two important properties: one representing the client functions that get invoked when the server "calls" something on the client, the second one is the property representing the server and all its functionality that we can call from the client. Let's start by hooking up the client and its methods. Earlier, we implemented in the Hub sitting on the server a call to addMessage() with the message coming in from the client to notify other clients. Open up the index.js file we created. We will do some alterations since we no longer use a persistent connection, but a hub instead. The code snippet to be changed is as follows:

```
$scope.click = function () {
    chat.send($scope.message);
};
```

The following changes will be made in the code:

```
$scope.click = function () {
    chat.server.send($scope.message);
};
```

Then, we want to change the following code:

```
chat.received(function (data) {
    $scope.$apply(function () {
        $scope.messages = $scope.messages + "\n" + data;
    });
});
```

The changes made in the code snippet are as follows:

```
chat.client.addMessage = function (message) {
    $scope.$apply(function () {
        $scope.messages = $scope.messages + "\n" + message;
    });
};
```

6. Your entire controller file should look as follows:

```
"use strict";
$application.controller("index", ["$scope", "chat", function
($scope, chat) {
    $scope.messages = "Connected";

    $scope.click = function () {
```

```
                chat.server.send($scope.message);
        };

        chat.client.addMessage = function (message) {
            $scope.$apply(function () {
                $scope.messages = $scope.messages + "\n" + message;
            });
        };
    }]);
```

Life cycle events

With hubs, there is a full set of events you can subscribe to, to deal with the life cycle.

The events you have are as follows:

```
connectionSlow
reconnecting
reconnected
disconnected
```

All of these events can be useful, not only for your application but also for notifying the user as to what is going on. This is especially true for slow connections and disconnected:

```
$.connection.hub.connectionSlow(function() {
    // Notify user about slow connection
});
$.connection.hub.disconnected(function() {
    // Notify user about being disconnected
});
```

For disconnected connections, you might want to retry connecting after a certain amount of time out; for instance, after 5 seconds:

```
$.connection.hub.disconnected(function() {
    setTimeout(function() {
        $.connection.hub.start();
    }, 5000);
});
```

Separation

One of the benefits we can already see with decoupling is that I changed the controller without it affecting the view in any way, nor did I have to do anything special, other than what was already going on. It's also easier to change it as the code is more focused on its part of the system, logic for the frontend, rather than focusing on other concerns. Typically, with a more classic jQuery approach to the problem, you would be querying the DOM for objects to get the data back and forth between view and logic. The queries are in the format of CSS selectors, and you would typically either query the elements by their name or by a CSS construct, leading to the entire system being coupled together with changes done in CSS or the DOM to change the JavaScript code. This is in the long run, and surprisingly maybe not even that long, hard to maintain, and leads to stale solutions that are so hard to change that you simply don't do it because it's too expensive.

Next, we'll see even more separation and how we can use AngularJS and its capabilities to deal with breaking things into the smallest problem and then putting it back together in a larger composition.

Summary

Exposing our functionality through hubs makes it easier to consume on the client, at least on JavaScript based clients, due to the proxy generation. It basically brings it to the client as if it was on the client. With the hub, you also get the ability to call the client from the server in a more natural manner. We've also seen how focused and more maintainable our code gets in the client. One of the things often important for applications is the ability to filter out messages so you only get messages relevant for your context. In the next chapter, groups will cover this; groups is the technique used in SignalR to accomplish this.

4
Groups

This chapter will cover how you can group connections together and target specific groups when sending messages. There will be times when you won't want to broadcast all messages to all clients; groups can help you send messages to the specific groups of connections. SignalR maintains which connections are in what groups, making it very easy to achieve. Groups allows you to join connections. When you are sending a message from the server, you can send it to a specific group by its group name, and only the connections in that group will receive the message, not the other connections.

In this chapter, we will cover the following topics:

- Establishing groups on the server
- Sending messages from the client to specific groups
- Receiving messages from the server about the added groups
- Composing your UI using AngularJS.

At this stage, the developer should be able to create groups, and put connections into these groups, and have a more maintainable frontend solution.

Getting specific with groups

Many scenarios require you to not be broadcasting to everyone, but to be more specific in who receives the message. SignalR provides an abstraction called groups for these. Groups hold the connections that will receive messages. The API for sending messages is the same, but you just choose to go to a specific group instead of going to everyone.

For our chat applications, we want to use groups to create chat rooms; specific groups will receive chat messages that none of the other rooms/groups will receive. In order for us to get this working, we will need to change our application slightly as follows:

1. First, we will need a class to manage the chat rooms that get created by any clients, so we keep track of them for any other clients that connect.

2. Right-click on the project and select **Add | New Item**. In the dialog box, select **Class** and give it a name `ChatRooms.cs`:

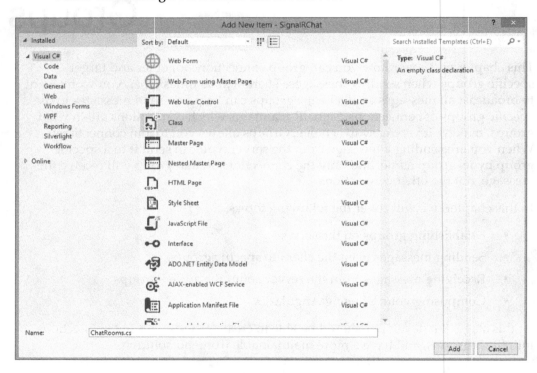

3. Basically, this class will just hold a list of strings that represent the different chat rooms by name for now:

```
Static List<string> _rooms = new List<string>();
```

4. We then want to have the ability to add and get all the rooms from it, and also to check whether a room already exists. By default, we will also add a well-known chat room called Lobby. The class should look like the following:

```
using System.Collections.Generic;

namespace SignalRChat
{
    public class ChatRooms
    {
        static List<string> _rooms = new List<string>();

        static ChatRooms()
        {
            _rooms.Add("Lobby");
        }

        public static void Add(string name)
        {
            _rooms.Add(name);
        }

        public static bool Exists(string name)
        {
            return _rooms.Contains(name);
        }

        public static IEnumerable<string> GetAll()
        {
            return _rooms;
        }
    }
}
```

The implementation uses a regular `List<string>` that is not thread-safe. This means that you can run into exceptions if you have two users joining a chat room at the same time. There are implementations out there that deal with this, and a quick search on the phrase `ConcurrentList` C# will yield a few implementations. Also, there is a `SynchronizedCollection<>` type, found in `System.Collections.Generics` after adding a reference to `System.ServiceModel`, that can be used.

1. Now, let's go back to the hub we created in *Chapter 3, Hubs*; in the `Chat.cs` file. We will need to add some new functionality to this class, and also change some existing to make it support the chat rooms. First, lets start by adding a method that we can call from the client in order to create a chat room:

    ```
    public void CreateChatRoom(string room)
    {
        if (!ChatRooms.Exists(room))
        {
            ChatRooms.Add(room);
            Clients.All.addChatRoom(room);
        }
    }
    ```

    The next thing we want to add is the support for clients to be able to join a room and receive any messages published to it. This is where we use the `Groups` property from the `Hub`, and add the connection of the client connected to the group with the same name as the room that we want to join:

    ```
    public void Join(string room)
    {
        Groups.Add(Context.ConnectionId, room);
    }
    ```

    With this, the client will only receive messages for the groups that it is part of, and none of the others.

2. Now that we have a subsystem to deal with rooms, and clients can connect to these rooms, we want to be able to tell the clients getting connected which rooms are available. On the `Hub`, there is a virtual method that we can override to get notified when a client gets connected: `OnConnected()`. There are also other methods for when clients disconnect and reconnect. However, for now, we only need the `OnConnected()` method. In this method, we basically get all the rooms that have been created, and we send them off to the client that got connected using the `Caller` property on the `Clients` property sitting on the `Hub`:

    ```
    public override Task OnConnected()
    {
    ```

```
    foreach (var room in ChatRooms.GetAll())
        Clients.Caller.addChatRoom(room);

    Join("Lobby");

return base.OnConnected();
}
```

3. We now need to change the `Send` method on the `Hub` as follows:

```
public void Send(string room, string message)
{
    Clients.Group(room).addMessage(message);
}
```

4. Your `Hub` should now look as follows:

```
public class Chat : Hub
{
    public void Join(string room)
    {
        Groups.Add(Context.ConnectionId, room);
    }

    public void CreateChatRoom(string room)
    {
        if (!ChatRooms.Exists(room))
        {
            ChatRooms.Add(room);
            Clients.All.addChatRoom(room);
        }
    }

    public void Send(string room, string message)
    {
        Clients.Group(room).addMessage(room, message);
    }

    public override Task OnConnected()
    {
        foreach (var room in ChatRooms.GetAll())
            Clients.Caller.addChatRoom(room);
        System.Console.WriteLine("Connected");
        return base.OnConnected();
    }

    public override Task OnDisconnected(bool stopCalled)
    {
        return base.OnDisconnected(stopCalled);
    }
}
```

The OnDisconnected override is not needed in this sample, but it shows how you can override it as well.

Composing the UI

Decoupling should be done at all levels, so the frontend is not excluded from this. Instead of thinking end-to-end in one view, we divide things up and create features in isolation. These features are specialized in doing one thing and one thing only. This makes the individual features expert in their isolated domain, instead of trying to fit everything in a wider feature. This creates something that is more decoupled and more maintainable. It's easier to change each of these features to become even better at what they do, without worrying about breaking other features. Typically, you could divide a page up as shown in the following screenshot:

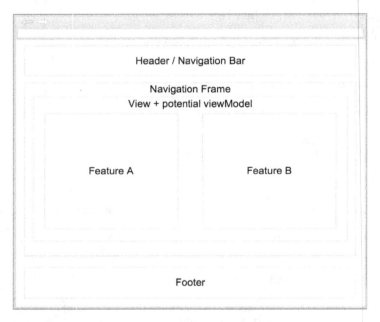

Every box represents a section of the system holding a feature. Each individual feature is put together in the larger composition.

One could create the preceding entire composition in one page and one code file, but it would be running the risk of being highly coupled together, and changing anything could easily break things that one didn't mean to touch at all.

In AngularJS, there are a few ways of doing compositions, and they all boil down to a single construct sitting at the core called directive. AngularJS directives are one of the most powerful features of AngularJS; it allows you to create your own custom directives that can act as attributes on elements, or even your own custom element. Angular will make sure to call the correct code when your directive is being used in the markup, and you're free to do whatever you want. Although there are some ways of achieving what we want to achieve, we are going to build an Angular directive that enables us to specify on an element that the content should come from another file:

1. Open up `config.js` and add the following code before the `global.$application` declaration:

```
application.directive("feature", ["$sce", function ($sce) {
    return {
        templateUrl: function (element, attributes) {
            return $sce.trustAsHtml(attributes.feature);
        }
    }
}]);
```

   This introduces a directive called feature. We're going to use this as an attribute, and we will, therefore, get the attribute value and pass it into something called **Strict Contextual Escaping (SCE)** that will make sure to render the given file securely.

2. AngularJS will take any dependencies that are resolved, and cache these as what is known as **singletons**. This means there is only one instance throughout the life cycle of your app. For our hubs, this means that by breaking our application up into smaller parts, we're going to have to accommodate a little bit. In `config.js`, right after the `(function (global)` `{` declaration at the top, put in the following:

```
function makeClientProxyFunction(callback) {
    return function () {
        callback.apply(this, arguments);
    };
}

function client(callback) {
    var client = {};
    callback(client);

    for (var property in client) {
```

```
            var value = client[property];
            if (typeof value != "function") {
                continue;
            }

            this.on(property, makeClientProxyFunction(value));
        }
    };
```

3. In addition to this, in the `registerHubFactory()` function following this code, you should make sure we set the client to be the newly created `client()` function. This function should now look as follows:

```
function registerHubFactory($provide, hubName) {
    $provide.factory(hubName, function () {
        var proxy = $.connection.hub.createHubProxy(hubName);
        proxy.client = client;
        return proxy;
    });
}
```

By having this client function that we can call in the different places, we can now enable to late bind client functions without having to prepare everything before we start the hub. This is really convenient and we do not need to worry about order of initialization or similar anywhere else in our app. We will make use of this new functionality a bit later.

4. Moving to the `index.html` file of your web application, we want to do some changes and make use of our new directive. Open up the `index.html` file; inside the div marked with the class container and the div within that with the class of the row. Let's add the following:

```
<div class="col-xs-4" feature="chatRooms">
</div>
```

Notice the `feature` attribute on the `div`. This is making use of the directive we created in the **config.js** file.

The container block in your HTML file should look as follows:

```
<div class="container">
    <div class="row">
        <div class="col-md-4" feature="chatRooms">
        </div>
        <div class="col-md-4">
```

```
<textarea id="chatWindow" style="width:400px;
height:200px;" ng-model="messages"></textarea>

        <div class="form-inline">
            <div class="form-group">
                <label for="messageTextBox" class="control-
label">Message</label>
                <div class="input-group">
                    <input type="text" class="form-control"
id="messageTextBox" placeholder="Message" ng-model="message">
                </div>
                <button type="submit" class="btn btn-primary"
ng-click="click()">Send</button>
            </div>
        </div>
    </div>
</div>
```

5. We will now need to create a couple of files; one for the view that represents the chatRooms and one for holding the controller. Add a file called chatRooms.html in the root of your project.

6. Put the following HTML inside the newly created file:

```
<div ng-controller="chatRooms">
    <select size="2" style="width:200px; height:200px;" ng-
model="currentChatRoom" ng-change="selectionChanged(currentChatRo
om)" ng-options="room for room in rooms"></select>
    <div class="form-inline">
        <div class="form-group">
            <label for="messageTextBox" class="control-
label">Chatroom</label>
            <div class="input-group">
                <input type="text" class="form-control"
id="messageTextBox" placeholder="Chatroom" ng-model="chatRoom">
            </div>
            <button type="submit" class="btn btn-primary" ng-
click="createRoom()">Create room</button>
        </div>
    </div>
</div>
```

Notice the `ng-controller` attribute; this is in fact also a directive. It is at this point setting up a controller that we're going to use for this tag and its children. In AngularJS, this will create a new scope, inheriting the parent scope for bindings—which will enable a local scope for this tag for us to work with.

Also, it is worth mentioning that the `ng-model` directive in Angular, as we've used before, is what binds the result of a value change in an input. The result will be bounded back to the scope for the variable that we specify. Likewise, by going into the input, the `ng-model` directive will also make AngularJS get the value from the scope.

7. Now, we are going to need to create a controller for this. Add a file called `chatRooms.js` and add the following to it:

```
"use strict";
$application.controller("chatRooms", ["$scope", "chat", function
($scope, chat) {
}]);
```

8. With the controller in place, we're going to need to include it in our `index.html` file where we have our other script included. Add the following `script` tag after the `index.js` file is included:

```
<script src="chatRooms.js" type="text/javascript"></script>
```

9. Let's put some logic into the controller in `chatRoom.js`. Let's add the following to the scope so that all the bindings work:

```
$scope.currentChatRoom = "Lobby";
$scope.chatRoom = "";
$scope.rooms = [];
```

10. Whenever the user clicks on the create room button, a function gets called; put in the following function inside the controller:

```
$scope.createRoom = function () {
    chat.server.createChatRoom($scope.chatRoom);
    chat.server.join($scope.chatRoom);
    $scope.currentChatRoom = $scope.chatRoom;
    $scope.chatRoom = "";
    $scope.$emit("chatRoomChanged", room);
};
```

Notice the `$scope.$emit()` code as this is an important part. Due to the fact that we're dividing our application up into smaller parts and we don't want to let the parts know about each other, we publish a message saying that the chat room has changed—because after creating a room, it's natural to be on the room one has created. We will see later on that we will be subscribing to this.

11. Now, let's add a client function for when the chat rooms are added. Primarily, we want to know when others are adding chat rooms, but this will also work when we add. Add the following function to the controller:

```
chat.client(function (client) {
    client.addChatRoom = function (room) {
        $scope.$apply(function () {
            $scope.rooms.push(room);
        });
    }
});
```

Notice the usage of the new `client()` function that we added in `config.js`. This takes a callback that gives us a client object in which we can add our client-side functions to.

Another important aspect you'll notice is what we've already done once before: `$scope.$apply()`. This will make sure we get our changes that affects visuals actually done. It tells AngularJS to perform a digest of the rendering, including bindings and so on.

12. The last thing we're going to need in the controller is the function that we will be setting up to handle selection changes, typically when a user selects a room. Add the following function to the controller:

```
$scope.selectionChanged = function (room) {
    $scope.$emit("chatRoomChanged", room);
    chat.server.join(room);
};
```

13. Your entire file should look as follows:

```
"use strict";
$application.controller("chatRooms", ["$scope", "chat", function
($scope, chat) {
    $scope.currentChatRoom = "Lobby";
    $scope.chatRoom = "";
    $scope.rooms = [];

    $scope.selectionChanged = function (room) {
        $scope.$emit("chatRoomChanged", room);
        chat.server.join(room);
    };

    $scope.createRoom = function () {
```

```
            chat.server.createChatRoom($scope.chatRoom);
            chat.server.join($scope.chatRoom);
            $scope.currentChatRoom = $scope.chatRoom;
            $scope.chatRoom = "";
            $scope.$emit("chatRoomChanged", $scope.chatRoom);
        };

        chat.client(function (client) {
            client.addChatRoom = function (room) {
                $scope.$apply(function () {
                    $scope.rooms.push(room);
                });
            }
        });
}]);
```

14. Now, we're going to need to change the main controller in `index.js`. First, we're going to need a third dependency in our definition that we're going to take in `$rootScope`. This enables us to subscribe to messages that bubbles up from any other features on the page. Make the definition look like the following:

```
$application.controller("index", ["$scope", "chat", "$rootScope",
function ($scope, chat, $rootScope) {
```

15. Now, we want a variable to hold the current chat room that we're on. At the top of the controller, add the following line:

```
var currentChatRoom = "Lobby";
```

16. Since we changed the signature of the `Send()` method on the hub, we are going to have to change the client as well to send the chat room the message is for. Make the click handler look like the following:

```
$scope.click = function () {
    chat.server.send(currentChatRoom, $scope.message);
};
```

17. Since the other feature is the publishing of a message when the user selects a different room, we want to subscribe to this message and change our own state accordingly. The `$rootScope` object will help us achieve this. Add the following code to the controller:

```
$rootScope.$on("chatRoomChanged", function (args, room) {
    currentChatRoom = room;
});
```

18. The entire controller should look as follows:

```
"use strict";
$application.controller("index", ["$scope", "chat", "$rootScope",
function ($scope, chat, $rootScope) {
    var currentChatRoom = "Lobby";

    $scope.messages = "Connected";

    $scope.click = function () {
        chat.server.send(currentChatRoom, $scope.message);
    };

    $rootScope.$on("chatRoomChanged", function (args, room) {
        currentChatRoom = room;
    });

    chat.client(function (client) {
        client.addMessage = function (message) {
            $scope.$apply(function () {
                $scope.messages = $scope.messages + "\n" +
message;
            });
        }
    });
}]);
```

Running the application should yield the following result:

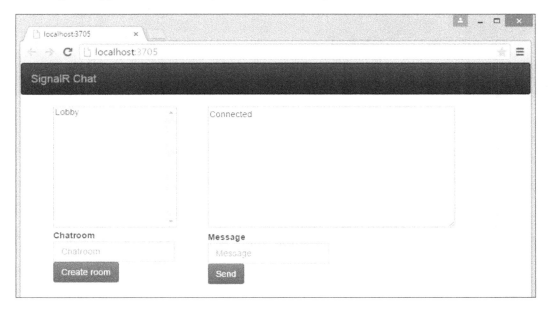

Summary

Often, you find yourself not wanting to broadcast your messages to all of your clients; the groups in SignalR gives you the control you want for grouping connections together and for only sending messages to the group(s) you want. You should now be able to apply grouping as a technique for filtering. Building applications larger than your average Hello World application often demands a certain amount of structure. Breaking things up into smaller problems instead of looking at an application as one big problem helps during development and maintenance. We've seen techniques for doing this with AngularJS creating our own directive. Directives are by far where the gold is hidden within AngularJS. It helps you tackle the problem of breaking things up, and encapsulating into reusable components, as well as breaking features up. You then compose this back into a bigger application. If you do things right, you'll also see that the features don't even need to know about each other, hence, gaining flexibility in how the composition is done. You can mix and match, and maybe even to a certain degree leave things up to the user as to what they want on the screen. One thing to consider for improvement is to encapsulate the main chat as a feature on its own and include this in the main page as part of the composition.

In the next chapter, we're going to look at how we can maintain the state across each call going back and forth from the client to the server.

5
State

At one level, applications need to keep data that puts the application in a certain state. Traditionally, this data is kept either in memory on the server or on the client and gets passed around between the client and the server, and often front and center in the calls as parameters. This chapter will cover how you can have a state in the client that is available automatically on the server. This type of state is then included in every round-trip taken between the client and the server as the result of a method invocation.

In this chapter, the following topics will be covered:

- Setting a state on the client that will be round-tripped
- Setting a state on the server that will be round-tripped

At this stage, the developer should be able to have a state on the client that is also on the server and that round-trips on every call in a transparent manner.

Becoming stateful

SignalR brings a lot to the table for abstractions; we've seen so far the abstractions of persistent connections and Hubs. Diving further into Hubs you'll see that there is even more. One of the cool things one can add is a round-tripped state. This is the state that is carried alongside any traffic going from a client to the server. So whenever you call something from the client to the server or the server calls something on the client, any state you have specified will be transferred along with the call being made. This is something that will be really convenient, especially when you have information that is not necessarily relevant for the method you need to call, but something that you might want to have cross cutting any method you call.

A great example of this, which we will use in this chapter, is the current chat room the user is on. Instead of having to maintain the state manually on the client, we can simply add it to the connection and it will round-trip between the server and the client. This also makes it possible for the server to change the state to something that would be much more involved, if not using this feature.

For now, we're just going to use it for something very simple—to keep track of the current chat room for the client. This way we don't need to have it on the method call for sending a message, it will just be available on the server as well as on the client. Perform the following steps to become stateful:

1. Let's start by changing the server a bit. Open the server-side representation of the Hub—Chat.cs.

2. Change the method signature by removing the first parameter for room that we put in the previous chapter:

   ```
   public void Send(string message)
   ```

3. Then, add the line for getting the current chat room from the caller's state. The method should look as follows:

   ```
   public void Send(string message)
   {
       var room = (string)Clients.Caller.currentChatRoom;
       Clients.Group(room).addMessage(message);
   }
   ```

 Note that it is important to cast currentChatRoom to a string for the call to the Group() method to work. Otherwise, the dynamic binder in the runtime will throw an exception.

4. When we join a room, we also want the server to set the current chat room from the server; change the join() method to look as follows:

   ```
   public void Join(string room)
   {
       Clients.Caller.currentChatRoom = room;
       Groups.Add(Context.ConnectionId, room);
   }
   ```

The client

That's all we will to do on the server for now. However, it is worth mentioning that any state can be written; it's not just to get the state from the client to the server. Also, as you've already seen, the `Caller` property is of a dynamic type, so you can put anything on it and it will just be there on the client. Right now, we have no way of knowing which room is the current room down into a chat:

1. Let's start by adding a functionality to the frontend that makes it easier to see what room you're on. Open the `index.js` file. Let's change the variable we have for holding `currentChatRoom` to a variable on the scope that we can use for binding:

   ```
   $scope.currentChatRoom = "Lobby";
   ```

2. Secondly, we want to change the message handling of the `chatRoomChanged` message; make the function look as follows:

   ```
   $rootScope.$on("chatRoomChanged", function (args, room) {
       $scope.currentChatRoom = room;
   });
   ```

    As the variable is now available in the scope, we can utilize it during binding.

3. Open the `index.html` file and let's make it clear above the text area as to which room we're on. Add the following before the `<textarea/>` tag:

   ```
   <b>Current room : {{currentChatRoom}}</b>
   ```

4. Let's make the text area slightly smaller in height. Set the height to `180px` instead of `200px`. This should make it aligned.

Running this now should give you **Current room** as a headline above the text area.

5. Open the chatRoom.js file. Let's change the first initialization line in the controller. In addition to setting the currentChatRoom variable on the scope, we want the client to set the state on the hub for it as well. Make the line look as follows:

```
chat.state.currentChatRoom = $scope.currentChatRoom = "Lobby";
```

> The state object on a hub proxy can hold any state. Anything you put in here will be round-tripped between the client and the server. The state is obviously for the connected client, so not any global state.

6. Move back to the index.js file. We will have to change the click function we set up on the scope. Since we no longer need the room as the first argument going into the send method on the server, we simply want to remove this. Make the function look as follows:

```
$scope.click = function () {
    chat.server.send($scope.message);
};
```

7. Now that we have the current chat room sitting as a state on all our calls to the chat hub, we can also implement a way of logging out of a chat room when we're joining one. Make the `Join` method, on the chat Hub in C#, look as follows:

```
public void Join(string room)
{
    var currentChatRoom = (string)Clients.Caller.currentChatRoom;
    if (!string.IsNullOrEmpty(currentChatRoom))
        Groups.Remove(Context.ConnectionId, currentChatRoom);

    Clients.Caller.currentChatRoom = room;
    Groups.Add(Context.ConnectionId, room);
}
```

Lifetime event handlers and more

The state's information is not available in any of the lifetime event handlers such as `OnConnected`, `OnDisconnected`, or `OnReconnected`. It only applies to methods on the server representation or functions on the client representation.

The type of state that you typically have should be large pieces of data; it is meant for simple things that are considered crosscutting in nature as it is round-tripped for every invocation.

In VB.NET or strongly typed Hubs, there is another property instead of `Caller` that you have to use; a new property called `CallerState` can be used for those scenarios.

Summary

From time to time there are bits of information that one could centralize and not have to pass along on all function and method calls. As shown in this chapter, the current chat room is a good example of such a state. You should now be able to add state that round-trips from the server to the client and give you back the opportunity to simplify your own code. Moving on, in the next chapter, we're going to look at securing your application and Hubs.

6
Security

This chapter will cover how you can secure your SignalR connections, which require authentication and authorization from the client, and also how you can communicate this back to the client in a graceful manner.

In this chapter, we will cover the following topics:

- General infrastructure needed to secure any web application
- Creating a login page and using AJAX calls to perform the actual login
- How to keep users' authentication for your connection
- How to have a specific role for your connection

At this stage, the developer should be familiar with securing their SignalR connections.

Locking things down

Security is something all applications need to have a relationship with, in one way or another. For instance, let's look at the type of chat application we're building. You might want to have private chat rooms or the entire chat to be private. You might have operations that are only allowed by users of a certain role. Luckily, SignalR has out-of-the-box support for the most common scenarios, and is very extensible if you'd like more complex solutions than the ones that are out-of-the-box. This chapter will take you through enabling forms authentication, a common scenario for applications. You could use Windows authentication and others as well, but for our application, we're using forms. In this chapter, we're hand-rolling everything ourselves; it will give you an idea of what is happening for security. As an alternative, you could go for something such as ASP.NET Identity. The way that you secure your SignalR artifacts would still be the same.

Putting the infrastructure in place

First of all, since our web application is built from HTML files and not ASPX or ASP. NET MVC controllers, we need to be able to have security in place for these as well, so we get redirected to a login page when not authenticated. There are a couple of approaches one can choose in order to make the security pipeline of ASP.NET kick in for static files such as HTML files; one of the approaches could be to enable all the HTTP modules to run for all the requests, but that would mean a potential performance hit for static content. So instead, we're going to tell ASP.NET to deal with the `.html` files specifically:

1. We will need to do a few changes to the `Web.config` file sitting in the web project to accomplish this. In the `compilation` tag sitting at the top, we need to add the page build providers for the extensions we want to support:

```
<compilation debug="true" targetFramework="4.5">
  <buildProviders>
    <add extension=".html" type="System.Web.Compilation.
PageBuildProvider"/>
  </buildProviders>
</compilation>
```

2. At the bottom-right before the end of the `<configuration>` tag, we will be adding a web server section, which is specific to **IIS7** and higher, to configure pretty much the same as we did for compilation:

```
<system.webServer>
  <handlers>
    <add name="HTML"
         path="*.html"
         verb="GET, HEAD, POST, DEBUG"
         type="System.Web.UI.PageHandlerFactory"
         resourceType="Unspecified"
         requireAccess="Script"
         />
  </handlers>
</system.webServer>
```

3. Then, inside the `<system.web>` tag again, right below the `compilation` tag, we will be adding our security. First, we set the authentication to be `Forms` and then add a form for our application with some attributes configuring its behavior; also, we add in an `authorization` tag denying all anonymous users, but allowing all the logged-in users:

```
<authentication mode="Forms">
  <forms name=".signalRChat"
```

```
              loginUrl="login.html"
              protection="All"
              path="/"
              timeout="30"/>
</authentication>

<authorization>
  <deny users="?"/>
  <allow users="*"/>
</authorization>
```

HTTP handler config

In order for the user to be authenticated, we need something we can call on the server to do the authentication. We could have gone with a hub for that purpose, or even a persistent connection. However, it would lead to some interesting configuration and having to disconnect from SignalR, when we were authenticated, and then having to reconnect. So instead, we can do something in the simplest possible way.

In order to be able to log in from our login page that we will be creating, we will be using an HTTP handler for authenticating and giving us the authentication cookie for any subsequent requests. We'll create the handler shortly. However, for now, let's just configure it to allow requests even if we're not logged in:

1. Add the following right before the `<system.webserver>` tag in `web.config`:

```
<location path="SecurityHandler.ashx">
  <system.web>
    <authorization>
      <allow users="*"/>
    </authorization>
  </system.web>
</location>
```

2. To enable us to include SignalR on the login page, we're also going to have to add a location section for the SignalR proxy path. Add the following right after the previous location section:

```
<location path="signalr">
  <system.web>
    <authorization>
      <allow users="*"/>
    </authorization>
  </system.web>
</location>
```

3. Your `web.config` should now look as follows:

```xml
<?xml version="1.0" encoding="utf-8"?>
<configuration>

  <system.web>
    <compilation debug="true" targetFramework="4.5">
      <buildProviders>
        <add extension=".html" type="System.Web.Compilation.
PageBuildProvider"/>
        <add extension=".htm" type="System.Web.Compilation.
PageBuildProvider"/>
      </buildProviders>
    </compilation>

    <httpRuntime targetFramework="4.5" />

    <authentication mode="Forms">
      <forms name=".signalRChat" loginUrl="login.html"
protection="All" path="/" timeout="30"/>
    </authentication>

    <authorization>
      <deny users="?"/>
      <allow users="*"/>
    </authorization>
  </system.web>

  <location path="SecurityHandler.ashx">
    <system.web>
      <authorization>
        <allow users="*"/>
      </authorization>
    </system.web>
  </location>

  <location path="signalr">
    <system.web>
      <authorization>
        <allow users="*"/>
      </authorization>
    </system.web>
  </location>

  <system.webServer>
    <handlers>
      <add name="HTML"
           path="*.html"
           verb="GET, HEAD, POST, DEBUG"
           type="System.Web.UI.PageHandlerFactory"
```

```
                    resourceType="Unspecified"
                    requireAccess="Script"
                    />

          <add name="HTM"
                    path="*.htm"
                    verb="GET, HEAD, POST, DEBUG"
                    type="System.Web.UI.PageHandlerFactory"
                    resourceType="Unspecified"
                    requireAccess="Script"
                    />
          </handlers>
     </system.webServer>
</configuration>
```

Authentication

Now that we have the configuration in place for securing our site properly, we want
to be able to actually log into the site:

1. Let's add the security handler that we just configured. Right-click on the web
    project and navigate to **Add** | **New** item. Select **Web** and then select **Generic
    Handler**. Give it the name SecurityHandler.ashx:

2. We will, for simplicity, be hardcoding our users, passwords, and roles. At the top of the `SecurityHandler.ashx` file, add the following:

```
Dictionary<string, string> _usersAndPassword = new
Dictionary<string, string>
{
    { "SomeCreator", "1234" },
    { "SomeChatter", "1234" }
};

Dictionary<string, string[]> _usersAndRoles = new
Dictionary<string, string[]>
{
    { "SomeCreator", new[] { "Creator" } }
};
```

3. Let's go ahead and add the simple authentication methods for dealing with the users. The authentication will result in a `FormsAuthentication` cookie that we will generate in the `AuthenticateUser` method that follows. The cookie will hold the username and all the roles for the user:

```
bool IsValidUser(string userName, string password)
{
    foreach (var user in _usersAndPassword.Keys)
        if (user.ToLowerInvariant() == userName.
ToLowerInvariant())
            if (_usersAndPassword[user] == password)
                return true;

    return false;
}

string[] GetRolesForUser(string userName)
{
    foreach (var user in _usersAndRoles.Keys)
        if (user.ToLowerInvariant() == userName.
ToLowerInvariant())
            return _usersAndRoles[user];

    return new string[0];
}

void AuthenticateUser(
    HttpContext context,
```

```
    string userName,
    params string[] roles)
{
    var ticket = new FormsAuthenticationTicket(1, userName,
        DateTime.Now,
        DateTime.Now.AddMinutes(30),
        false,
        string.Join(";", roles));
    var cookieString = FormsAuthentication.Encrypt(ticket);
    var cookie = new HttpCookie(FormsAuthentication.
FormsCookieName, cookieString);
    context.Response.Cookies.Add(cookie);
}
```

4. The handler will need an implementation in `ProcessRequest()` that deals with the incoming authentication. Again, for simplicity, we will be using clear text passwords sitting inside a HTTP form. Of course, it's recommended to do something a bit more involved than this, especially if you're not using SSL to secure your connection:

```
public void ProcessRequest(HttpContext context)
{
    var userName = context.Request.Form["userName"];
    var password = context.Request.Form["password"];

    if (IsValidUser(userName, password))
    {
        var roles = GetRolesForUser(userName);
        AuthenticateUser(context, userName, roles);
        context.Response.StatusCode = (int)HttpStatusCode.OK;
    }
    else
    {
        context.Response.StatusCode = (int)HttpStatusCode.
Forbidden;
    }
}
```

5. The entire `SecurityHandler` class should look as follows:

```
using System;
using System.Collections.Generic;
using System.Linq;
using System.Net;
using System.Web;
```

```
using System.Web.Security;

namespace SignalRChat
{
    /// <summary>
    /// Summary description for SecurityHandler
    /// </summary>
    public class SecurityHandler : IHttpHandler
    {
        Dictionary<string, string> _usersAndPassword = new
Dictionary<string, string>
        {
            { "SomeCreator", "1234" },
            { "SomeChatter", "1234" }
        };

        Dictionary<string, string[]> _usersAndRoles = new
Dictionary<string, string[]>
        {
            { "SomeCreator", new[] { "Creator" } }
        };

        bool IsValidUser(string userName, string password)
        {
            foreach (var user in _usersAndPassword.Keys)
                if (user.ToLowerInvariant() == userName.
ToLowerInvariant())
                    if (_usersAndPassword[user] == password)
                        return true;

            return false;
        }

        string[] GetRolesForUser(string userName)
        {
            foreach (var user in _usersAndRoles.Keys)
                if (user.ToLowerInvariant() == userName.
ToLowerInvariant())
                    return _usersAndRoles[user];

            return new string[0];
        }
```

```
        void AuthenticateUser(
            HttpContext context,
            string userName,
            params string[] roles)
        {
            var ticket = new FormsAuthenticationTicket(1,
userName,
                DateTime.Now,
                DateTime.Now.AddMinutes(30),
                false,
                string.Join(";", roles));
            var cookieString = FormsAuthentication.
Encrypt(ticket);
            var cookie = new HttpCookie(FormsAuthentication.
FormsCookieName, cookieString);
            context.Response.Cookies.Add(cookie);
        }


        public void ProcessRequest(HttpContext context)
        {
            var userName = context.Request.Form["userName"];
            var password = context.Request.Form["password"];

            if (IsValidUser(userName, password))
            {
                var roles = GetRolesForUser(userName);
                AuthenticateUser(context, userName, roles);
                context.Response.StatusCode = (int)HttpStatusCode.
OK;
            }
            else
            {
                context.Response.StatusCode = (int)HttpStatusCode.
Forbidden;
            }
        }

        public bool IsReusable
        {
            get
            {
                return false;
            }
        }
    }
```

6. Now, we will need a page where we can log in. This is the page we configured in `web.config` as the redirect URL when users try to access the site. Right-click on the web project, navigate to **Add | New Item**, select **Web**, and then select **HTML page**. Name the page `login.html`.

7. As we did with the index file, we want to include Bootstrap to make things look good. Inside the `<head>` tag, add the following:

```
<link href="Content/bootstrap.min.css" rel="stylesheet" />
<link href="Content/bootstrap-theme.min.css" rel="stylesheet" />
```

8. In the page, we will add a form inside the body holding the input for the authentication. This could also have been a form pointing directly to the `SecurityHandler`, but we will be doing this programmatically instead. Add the following `<body>` tag:

```
<div class="container">
    <div class="row">
        <div class="col-xs-8">
            <form class="form-horizontal">
                <div class="form-group">
                    <h1 class="col-sm-2 control-label">Login</h1>
                </div>
                <div class="form-group">
                    <label for="inputEmail3" class="col-sm-2
control-label">Email</label>
                    <div class="col-sm-10">
                        <input type="text" class="form-control"
id="inputEmail3" placeholder="Email" data-ng-model="userName">
                    </div>
                </div>
                <div class="form-group">
                    <label for="inputPassword3" class="col-sm-2
control-label">Password</label>
                    <div class="col-sm-10">
                        <input type="password" class="form-
control" id="inputPassword3" placeholder="Password" data-ng-
model="password">
                    </div>
                </div>
                <div class="form-group">
                    <div class="col-sm-offset-2 col-sm-10">
                        <button type="submit" class="btn btn-
default" data-ng-click="signIn()">Sign in</button>
                    </div>
```

```
                </div>
            </form>
        </div>
    </div>
</div>
```

 As we've done in the earlier chapters, we're using the `data-ng-model` and `data-ng-click` directives to be able to bind the HTML to the scope and make it available for the JavaScript code.

9. Then, we go ahead and add the following scripts at the bottom of the `<body>` element:

```
<script src="Scripts/jquery-1.9.1.min.js" type="text/
javascript"></script>
<script src="Scripts/bootstrap.min.js" type="text/javascript"></
script>
<script src="Scripts/angular.js" type="text/javascript"></script>
<script src="Scripts/jquery.signalR-2.2.0.min.js"></script>
<script src="SignalR/Hubs" type="text/javascript"></script>

<script src="config.js" type="text/javascript"></script>
<script src="login.js" type="text/javascript"></script>
```

10. We now want to provide the JavaScript logic for this; the last script we included is a file called `login.js`, which does not exist yet. Add a new JavaScript file called `login.js`. Make it look as follows:

```
"use strict";
$application.controller("login", ["$scope", "$http", function
($scope, $http) {
    $scope.signIn = function () {
        $http({
            method: "POST",
            url: "/SecurityHandler.ashx",
            headers: { 'Content-Type': 'application/x-www-form-
urlencoded' },
            transformRequest: function (obj) {
                var str = [];
                for (var p in obj)
                    str.push(encodeURIComponent(p) + "=" +
encodeURIComponent(obj[p]));
                return str.join("&");
            },
```

```
                        data: {
                            userName: $scope.userName,
                            password: $scope.password
                        }
                }).success(function () {
                    window.location = "/";
                });
        }
    }]);
```

We're doing what is commonly known as an AJAX call for the authentication. AngularJS has an object called $http that we can use to work with this; we take this as a dependency and use it directly. We want to perform a HTTP POST with the username and password bound from the scope. To be able to do this, we have to set the header to be a form that is URL encoded. This is also why we have the transform request—to encode the content properly.

Running the chat should now lead you to the login page, and you will not be able to get to the index.html file.

Securing the hub

Since, by default, we have everything locked down, the hub is also protected. This means that going directly to the URL won't get you there. However, we will be explicitly securing the hub. SignalR comes with an attribute called **Authorize**, similar to the one you find in ASP.NET MVC and so on. There are other mechanisms for securing hubs, but we won't go into that in this book. To enforce that users need to be logged in, we can use the Authorize() attribute:

- The Authorize() attribute can be used for both hubs and methods on a hub. It has a couple of options that can be passed to it, such as users and roles holding comma delimited required users and/or roles. However, it also has a property called RequireOutgoing that tells SignalR what direction it should be securing. By default, it is only incoming, but by setting it to true, it will become outgoing. We will set it to true, so that we secure both directions; by effectively making it impossible for anyone to consume messages, you have to be authorized for both calling methods on the hub and getting messages from the hub:

```
[Authorize(RequireOutgoing=true)]
public class Chat : Hub
{
```

- In addition to requiring authenticated users for the hub, we will be adding a specific role requirement for the `CreateChatRoom()` method that sits on the hub:

```
[Authorize(Roles="Creator")]
public void CreateChatRoom(string room)
{
```

The great finale

Now, the final piece of the puzzle. SignalR uses the underlying credential information found on threads in .NET. This means we will have to populate this information based on the cookie generated by our security handler. For this, we're going to need **Global Application Class**. Right-click on the web project and navigate to **Add | New** item. Select **Web** and then select **Generic Handler**. Give it the name `Global.asax`:

1. If the request coming in is authenticated, we want to get the cookie and decrypt it. From this, we want to put the identity into the `HttpContext`. Open the `Global.asax.cs` file and make the `Application_AuthenticateRequest` method look like follows:

```
protected void Application_AuthenticateRequest(object sender,
EventArgs e)
{
    if( HttpContext.Current.User != null )
    {
        if( Request.IsAuthenticated == true )
        {
            var ticket = FormsAuthentication.Decrypt(
                Context.Request.Cookies[FormsAuthentication.
FormsCookieName].Value);
            var roles = ticket.UserData.Split(';');
            var id = new FormsIdentity(ticket);
            Context.User = new GenericPrincipal(id, roles);
        }
    }
}
```

2. Running the web app should now lead you straight to the `login.html` file. Log in as one of the users, such as `SomeCreator` and its password `1234`, and by logging in, you should be redirected to `index.html` where you can do everything you could before. Verify that everything is working by closing the browser and logging in as `SomeChatter` and try to create a new chat room; a new room should not appear.

Summary

Security is something that all applications must take into consideration. SignalR just taps into existing infrastructure, both for the client and the server side, making this possible. All we need to do is authenticate and use the infrastructure to our advantage to get our app secured. You should be able to apply security in the form described in this chapter, but also get an idea to move forward with even more security, such as applying SSL. The next big step now is to make our application scale. With the scaleout options of SignalR, one should be capable of truly scaling to any need.

The next chapter will go into depth on how to scale with different options, even into the cloud.

7
Scaling Out

This chapter will cover how to host SignalR in different environments. Some solutions out there need to be self-contained and not rely on any server setup; this chapter will show you how to do that, ranging all the way to larger solutions where you need to scale out into a multi-server environment and even all the way to the cloud. When one has multiple servers and is not necessarily controlling which server will be hit, we need to deal with this. In this chapter, we'll cover the following topics:

- The basics of messaging and how SignalR deals with them
- Using SQL Server for scaling out
- Using Azure Service Bus for scaling out
- Using Redis for scaling out
- Discussing how one can implement a bridge for their own messaging backplane

At this stage, the developer should be familiar with how the server works and how to set it up in their own app. They should have a working sample of the chat working with the OWIN server. The developer should also be familiar with how and why to scale out the messaging aspect of SignalR.

It's all about messages in SignalR

Underneath the covers, SignalR wraps all communication between the server and clients into messages holding all the information with its origin, what the message is for, and the content of the message. By default, these messages are kept in memory in the process that hosts your SignalR-based solution.

This means that having two servers will not have inter-process communication going on, so one client sitting on one server and another on a second one would not know about each other's messages. With the flexibility of SignalR at the core level of it dealing with this through well-defined interfaces, it is fairly simple to make it scale out for different technologies. This is something the SignalR team has done as well; they provide the ability to scale out in different ways. You get support to use Microsoft SQL Server for temporary storage of messages between servers, or use Windows Azure Service Bus to distribute the messages, or even the popular Redis to do this. There is a thriving community around SignalR and already a few more implementations for popular message buses and key/value stores to act as a backplane. Expect this to be a space that grows even more.

Scaling out with SQL Server

In your server project, you will need a package for the SQL scale-out option. Add a NuGet package reference to `Microsoft.AspNet.SignalR.SqlServer`. We are now ready to configure it. Open the `Startup.cs` file, before the call to `.RunSignalR()` or `.MapSignalR()` as we did in *Chapter 3*, *Hubs*, we will add the configuration for SQL Server.

Add the following code before it:

```
GlobalHost.DependencyResolver.UseSqlServer(
        "Data Source=(local);"+
        "Initial Catalog=SignalRChat;"+
        "Integrated Security=True"
    );
```

The overload we're using is one that takes a SQL Server connection string. It could be any SQL Server you have either on-premise or in the cloud.

In order for SignalR to be able to use SQL Server as a messaging backend, we need to enable something called a **Service Broker** for our database. After creating your database, right-click on it in the SQL Server Management Studio and then select **Properties**.

In the **Options** page, scroll down until you find the **Service Broker** section and enable the **Broker Enabled** flag, as shown here:

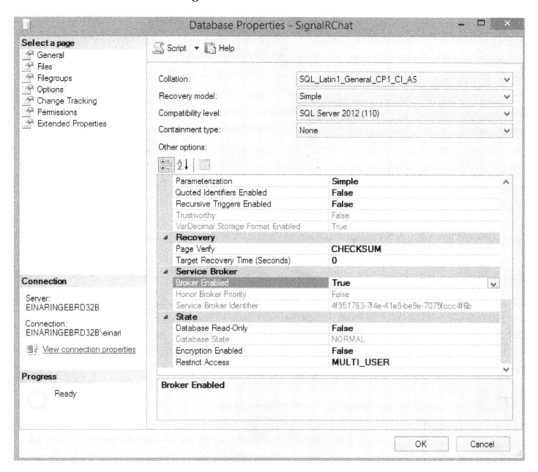

We should now be able to run our application and it will generate messages in the **dbo.SignalR_Messages** table, as shown here:

Scaling out with Redis

Redis is another option that can be used with SignalR for scaling out. Redis is an open source distributed key-value store. It is very popular in the Unix space, and has also been adopted by Microsoft. It's fairly easy to get running on Azure or other cloud options. If you want to try things out with Redis locally, the procedure is as follows:

Download the source that Microsoft has published through their Open Tech initiative on GitHub at `https://github.com/MSOpenTech/redis`. Follow the guide there, build and run it.

Once it is running, we can get going with configuring our chat application for Redis instead of the SQL solution.

Add a reference to the `Microsoft.AspNet.SignalR.Redis` NuGet package. As with SQL Server, adding Redis is just as easy. Go to the `Startup.cs` file, and instead of using the `.UseSqlServer()` method, replace it with the following:

```
GlobalHost.DependencyResolver.UseRedis(
    "localhost",
    6379,
    "",
    "signalr.key");
```

This points us to the local Redis server running with a blank password, something you obviously would not have in production.

Running the server with connected clients , you should see the result in the Redis console output directly:

```
C:\Users\einari\AppData\Local\Temp\Temp1_redisbin.zip\redis-server.exe        –  ☐  ✕
[5400] 06 Feb 21:57:11 - 0 clients connected (0 slaves), 444172 bytes in use
[5400] 06 Feb 21:57:16 - 0 clients connected (0 slaves), 444172 bytes in use
[5400] 06 Feb 21:57:21 - 0 clients connected (0 slaves), 444172 bytes in use
[5400] 06 Feb 21:57:26 - 0 clients connected (0 slaves), 444172 bytes in use
[5400] 06 Feb 21:57:31 - 0 clients connected (0 slaves), 444172 bytes in use
[5400] 06 Feb 21:57:36 - 0 clients connected (0 slaves), 444172 bytes in use
[5400] 06 Feb 21:57:41 - 0 clients connected (0 slaves), 444172 bytes in use
[5400] 06 Feb 21:57:46 - 0 clients connected (0 slaves), 444172 bytes in use
[5400] 06 Feb 21:57:51 - 0 clients connected (0 slaves), 444172 bytes in use
[5400] 06 Feb 21:57:56 - 0 clients connected (0 slaves), 444172 bytes in use
[5400] 06 Feb 21:58:01 - 0 clients connected (0 slaves), 444172 bytes in use
[5400] 06 Feb 21:58:06 - 0 clients connected (0 slaves), 444172 bytes in use
[5400] 06 Feb 21:58:11 - 0 clients connected (0 slaves), 444172 bytes in use
[5400] 06 Feb 21:58:16 - 0 clients connected (0 slaves), 444172 bytes in use
[5400] 06 Feb 21:58:21 - 0 clients connected (0 slaves), 444172 bytes in use
[5400] 06 Feb 21:58:26 - 0 clients connected (0 slaves), 444172 bytes in use
[5400] 06 Feb 21:58:31 - 0 clients connected (0 slaves), 444172 bytes in use
[5400] 06 Feb 21:58:36 - 0 clients connected (0 slaves), 444172 bytes in use
[5400] 06 Feb 21:58:41 - 0 clients connected (0 slaves), 444172 bytes in use
[5400] 06 Feb 21:58:46 - Accepted 127.0.0.1:1157
[5400] 06 Feb 21:58:46 - Accepted 127.0.0.1:1158
[5400] 06 Feb 21:58:46 - 2 clients connected (0 slaves), 460304 bytes in use
[5400] 06 Feb 21:58:51 - DB 0: 1 keys (0 volatile) in 4 slots HT.
[5400] 06 Feb 21:58:51 - 2 clients connected (0 slaves), 461748 bytes in use
```

Scaling out with Azure

A third option that's available out of the box is the usage of Azures Service Bus, a distributed messaging system for Microsoft's cloud solution—Azure. We will cover it briefly in this book as it requires you to have the Azure SDK installed to make it fully functional. Once you have installed the Azure SDK, you will need to add a cloud project to your solution and add the Web project as a website to the cloud project. When you have all that done, you need to set the cloud project as the startup project. The reasoning behind this is that it needs to be running inside the Azure emulator to be able to this, so it's relying on infrastructure to do this.

Log into your Windows Azure portal and go to **Service Bus**. From the top of the page, create a namespace if you haven't already done so:

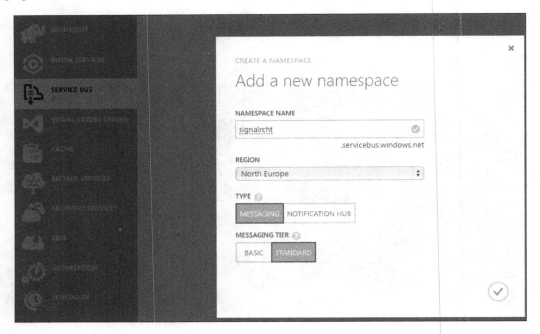

Navigate to the new namespace in the portal after creation. At the bottom of the page, you'll find a button called **Connection Information**; click on it.

You will find the connection string that we need in our code; copy it from the page so that you can add it in the code:

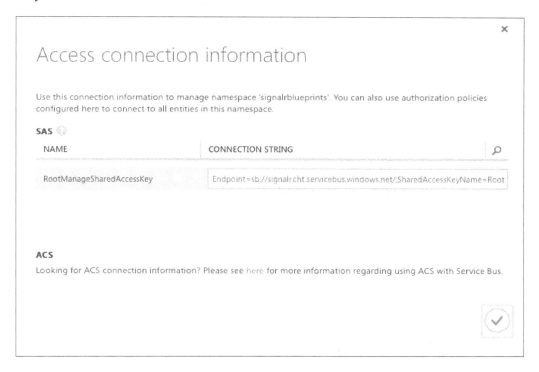

Back in Visual Studio, we're going to add a NuGet package reference called `Microsoft.AspNet.SignalR.ServiceBus` to the project. Open the `Startup.cs` file again and replace the `.UseRedis()` code with the following:

```
GlobalHost.DependencyResolver.UseServiceBus(
    "your connection string from azure",
    "signalr");
```

You should now be able to run your solution on Azure and be ready for scaling your solution any way you like.

Creating our own backplane

There are other scale-out solutions available out there as well. For instance, the community has created **RabbitMQ** support. Also, the popular **NServiceBus** has a backplane implementation for SignalR.

The scale-out mechanisms utilize what is known as a backplane. In electronics, a backplane is a group of parallel connectors. By analogy in SignalR talk, this means connecting to multiple servers. We need the backplane to be able to communicate in a multi server world.

However, you might have infrastructure in place that does not have any support yet or it is proprietary to your system. Fear not, implementing support is fairly easy. At the heart of it all sits an interface called `IMessageBus` that you can build on top of. However, for the most part, you probably don't even need all this raw power. You will only need an abstraction for the scale-out scenario called `ScaleoutMessageBus`. Let's have a look at how you can do this:

1. Add a C# class called `CustomBus` to the root of the project.

2. Make it inherit from `ScaleoutMessageBus`:

   ```
   using Microsoft.AspNet.SignalR.Messaging;

   namespace SignalRChat
   {
       public class CustomBus : ScaleoutMessageBus
       {
       }
   }
   ```

3. This won't compile, as the base class has dependencies on the constructor it needs to fulfill. One of these dependencies is a configuration object representing any configuration for your custom bus implementation. Let's create a C# class called `CustomBusConfiguration`:

   ```
   using Microsoft.AspNet.SignalR.Messaging;

   namespace SignalRChat
   {
       public class CustomBusConfiguration : ScaleoutConfiguration
       {
       }
   }
   ```

This configuration object is where you keep any specific configuration for your bus. In our sample, we're not really connecting to anything, so we won't put anything into it.

4. With the configuration type in place, we can now put in a constructor that can fulfill the dependencies of the base class for our message bus. Go back to the `CustomBus` class and add in the following constructor:

```
public CustomBus(IDependencyResolver dependencyResolver,
CustomBusConfiguration configuration)
    : base(dependencyResolver, configuration)
{
}
```

5. The next thing we will need is to tell the underlying bus implementation to open. Add the following into the constructor:

```
Open(0);
```

The `0` being passed in is the number of the queue to `open`.

6. Every message in the system has an identifier, `ulong` that should be incremental. You as an implementer of the custom bus need to keep track of this. Introduce a `static` variable on the class to hold this:

```
static ulong _messageId;
```

7. The `ScaleoutMessageBus` type has a few things we can override. We want to focus on the `Send()` method that gets invoked when a message is sent. There are other lifecycle methods also, subscription and topic-related methods that can be overridden and dealt with, but we're not going into those in this chapter. Put the following method in place:

```
protected override Task Send(int streamIndex, IList<Message>
messages)
{
    var scaleoutMessage = new ScaleoutMessage(messages);
    OnReceived(streamIndex, _messageId++, scaleoutMessage);
    return Task.FromResult(0);
}
```

The key to telling SignalR when a message is received is to use the `OnReceived()` method from the base class. In this sample, we call it directly from the `Send()` method, but this is the method you'd call when receiving a message from your actual backplane.

Worth noting is that everything is considered async in SignalR; therefore, it returns `Task`. Since we're not doing anything special, we basically return an empty `Task`.

Hooking it all up

With all the code to deal with the bus and messaging, we need to hook it up and make use of it. We'll do this in the same manner as other buses have been doing it:

1. Let's create extension methods for `DependencyResolver` as we've seen done with the SQL, Azure, and Redis implementations. Add a C# class called `DependencyResolverExtensions` and make it look as follows:

```
using System;
using Microsoft.AspNet.SignalR;
using Microsoft.AspNet.SignalR.Messaging;

namespace SignalRChat
{
    public static class DependencyResolverExtensions
    {
        public static IDependencyResolver UseCustom(this
IDependencyResolver resolver)
        {
            var bus = new Lazy<CustomBus>(() => new
CustomBus(resolver, new CustomBusConfiguration()));
            resolver.Register(typeof(IMessageBus), () => bus.
Value);

            return resolver;
        }
    }
}
```

   The `DependencyResolver` is the key to everything inside SignalR, and this code registers the relationship between `IMessageBus` and our implementation. So, whenever SignalR internally asks for an implementation of `IMessageBus`, it will get ours. We also want this to be initialized as late as possible; therefore, we use the `Lazy` type to wrap it.

2. Open the `Startup.cs` file and let's hook it all up. In the `Configuration` method, you can now add the following:

```
GlobalHost.DependencyResolver.UseCustom();
```

3. Add a breakpoint in the `Send()` method of the `CustomBus` class and run it with the debugger attached. You should hit the method and see something like the following:

```
protected override Task Send(int streamIndex, IList<Message> messages)
{
    var scaleoutMessage = new ScaleoutMessage(messages);
    OnReceived(streamIndex, _messageId++, scaleoutMessage);
    return Task.FromResult(0);
}
```

Summary

Working with a solution over multiple servers can easily become a nightmare. A state being kept in memory on one server is not available on the second, leading to weird scenarios as a result. Having a stateless server is vital in those scenarios and also when applying SignalR in a multi server environment. Hubs or persistent connections should not keep the state floating around locally on a server, but it should be architected in a way to accommodate the fact that you're running distributed environment. There is no guarantee as to what server the SignalR is connecting to, and also if the client needs to reconnect, so the scale-out option is absolutely vital to the story. With the different options described in this chapter, you should now be able to scale in an on-premise solution as well as in the cloud. Moving on to the next chapter, we'll see how we can take the same functionality that we've created for the web and make it in a WPF .NET client.

8
Building a WPF .NET Client

In this chapter, we will bring the full feature set of what we've built so far for the web onto the desktop through a WPF .NET client. There are quite a few ways of developing Windows client solutions, and WPF was introduced back in 2005 and has become one of the most popular ways of developing software for Windows. In WPF, we have something called XAML, which is what Windows Phone development supports and is also the latest programming model in Windows 10. In this chapter, the following topics will be covered:

- MVVM
- A brief introduction to the SOLID principles
- XAML
- WPF
- The C# approach to consume Hubs
- The C# approach to use groups

Decoupling it all

So you might be asking yourself, what is **MVVM**? It stands for **Model View ViewModel**: a pattern for client development that became very popular in the XAML stack, enabled by Microsoft based on Martin Fowlers presentation model (http://martinfowler.com/eaaDev/PresentationModel.html). Its principle is that you have a ViewModel that holds the state and exposes a behavior that can be utilized from a view. The view observes any changes of the state the ViewModel exposes, making the ViewModel totally unaware that there is a view.

The ViewModel is decoupled and can be put in isolation and is perfect for automated testing. As part of the state that the ViewModel typically holds is the model part, which is something it usually gets from the server, and a SignalR hub is the perfect transport to get this. It boils down to recognizing the different concerns that make up the frontend and separating it all.

This gives us the following diagram:

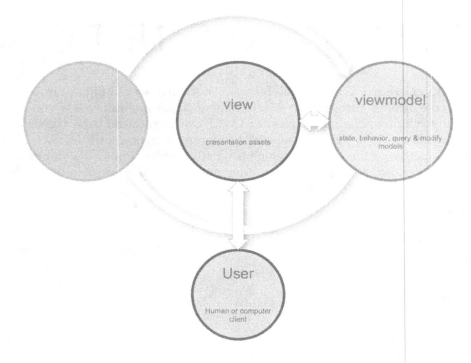

Decoupling – the next level

In this chapter, one of the things we will brush up is the usage of the **Dependency Inversion Principle**, the **D** of SOLID. Let's start with the first principle: the **S** in SOLID stands for **Single Responsibility Principle**, which states that a method or a class should only have one reason to change and only have one responsibility. With this, we can't have our units take on more than one responsibility and need help from collaborators to do the entire job. These collaborators are things we now depend on and we should represent these dependencies clearly to our units so that anyone or anything instantiating it knows what we are depending on. We have now flipped around the way in which we get dependencies. Instead of the unit trying to instantiate everything itself, we now clearly state what we need as collaborators, opening up for the calling code to decide what implementations of these dependencies you want to pass on. Also, this is an important aspect; typically, you'd want the dependencies expressed in the form of interfaces, yielding flexibility for the calling code. Basically, what this all means is that instead of a unit or system instantiating and managing its dependencies, we decouple and let something called as the Inversion of Control container deal with this. In the sample, we will use an **IoC (Inversion of Control)** container called **Ninject** that will deal with this for us. What it basically does is manage what implementations to give to the dependency specified on the constructor. Often, you'll find that the dependencies are interfaces in C#. This means one is not coupled to a specific implementation and has the flexibility of changing things at runtime based on configuration. Another role of the IOC container is to govern the life cycle of the dependencies. It is responsible for knowing when to create new instances and when to reuse an instance. For instance, in a web application, there are some systems that you want to have a life cycle of per request, meaning that we will get the same instance for the lifetime of a web request. The life cycle is configurable in what is known as a binding. When you explicitly set up the relationship between a contract (interface) and its implementation, you can choose to set up the life cycle behavior as well.

Building for the desktop

The first thing we will need is a separate project in our solution:

1. Let's add it by right-clicking on the solution in **Solution Explorer** and navigating to **Add | New Project**:

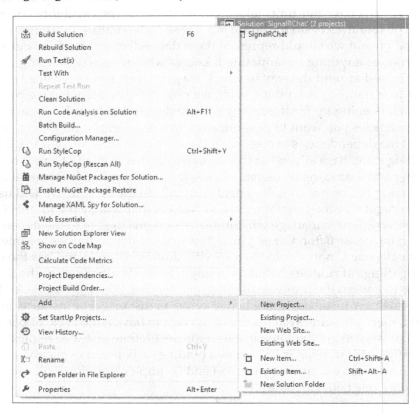

2. In the **Add New Project** dialog box, we want to make sure the **.NET Framework 4.5.1** is selected.

 We could have gone with 4.5, but some of the dependencies that we're going to use have switched to 4.5.1. This is the latest version of the .NET Framework at the time of writing, so if you can, use it.

3. Make sure to select **Windows Desktop** and then select **WPF Application**. Give the project the name `SignalRChat.WPF` and then click on the **OK** button:

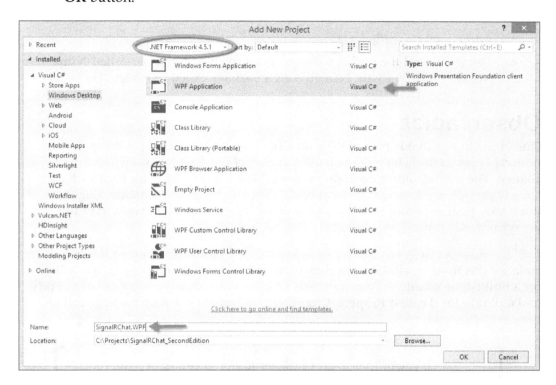

Setting up the packages

We will need some packages to get started properly. This process is described in detail in *Chapter 1, The Primer*. Let's start off by adding SignalR, which is our primary framework that we will be working with to move on. We will be pulling this using NuGet, as described in *Chapter 1, The Primer*:

1. Right-click on the **References** in **Solution Explorer** and select **Manage NuGet Packages**, and type `Microsoft.AspNet.SignalR.Client` in the Search dialog box. Select it and click on **Install**.

2. Next, we're going to pull down something called as **Bifrost**.

Bifrost is a library that helps us build MVVM-based solutions on WPF; there are a few other solutions out there, but we'll focus on Bifrost.

3. Add a package called `Bifrost.Client`.

4. Then, we need the package that gives us the IOC container called **Ninject**, working together with Bifrost. Add a package called `Bifrost.Ninject`.

Observables

One of the things that is part of WPF and all other XAML-based platforms is the notion of observables, be it in properties or collections that will notify when they change. The notification is done through well-known interfaces for this, such as `INotifyPropertyChanged` or `INotifyCollectionChanged`. Implementing these interfaces quickly becomes tedious all over the place where you want to notify everything when there are changes.

Luckily, there are ways to make this pretty much go away. We can generate the code for this instead, either at runtime or at build time. For our project, we will go for a build-time solution. To accomplish this, we will use something called as **Fody** and a plugin for it called **PropertyChanged**. Add another NuGet package called `PropertyChanged.Fody`.

If you happen to get problems during compiling, it could be the result of the dependency to a package called Fody not being installed. This happens for some versions of the package in combination with the latest Roslyn compiler. To fix this, install the NuGet package called Fody.

Now that we have all the packages, we will need some configuration in code:

1. Open the `App.xam.cs` file and add the following statement:

```
using Bifrost.Configuration;
```

2. The next thing we will need is a constructor for the `App` class:

```
public App()
{
    Configure.DiscoverAndConfigure();
}
```

This will tell Bifrost to discover the implementations of the well-known interfaces to do the configuration.

3. Bifrost uses the IoC container internally all the time, so the next thing we will need to do is give it an implementation. Add a class called `ContainerCreator` at the root of the project. Make it look as follows:

```
using Bifrost.Configuration;
using Bifrost.Execution;
using Bifrost.Ninject;
using Ninject;

namespace SignalRChat.WPF
{
    public class ContainerCreator : ICanCreateContainer
    {
        public IContainer CreateContainer()
        {
            var kernel = new StandardKernel();
            var container = new Container(kernel);
            return container;
        }
    }
}
```

 We've chosen Ninject among others that Bifrost supports, mainly because of familiarity and habit. If you happen to have another favorite, Bifrost supports a few. It's also fairly easy to implement your own support; just go to the source at http://github.com/dolittle/bifrost to find reference implementations.

4. In order for Bifrost to be targeting the desktop, we need to tell it through configuration. Add a class called `Configurator` at the root of the project. Make it look as follows:

```
using Bifrost.Configuration;

namespace SignalRChat.WPF
{
    public class Configurator : ICanConfigure
    {
```

```
            public void Configure(IConfigure configure)
            {
                configure.Frontend.Desktop();
            }
        }
    }
```

Adding security

As with the web solution, we will now need to log in, in order for us to do anything. In order for us to do that, we will need some client-side infrastructure and also the visuals to do the actual retrieval of the username and password.

Adding support for cookies

The security that we put in place on the web solution uses cookies to identify the user session. We will need to use this in the desktop as well. To make the cookies accessible, we will create an implementation of WebClient found in the .NET Framework that exposes a container for the cookies.

Create a new class called CookieAwareWebClient in the root of the project. Make the class look as follows:

```
using System;
using System.Net;

namespace SignalRChat.WPF
{
    public class CookieAwareWebClient : WebClient
    {
        public readonly CookieContainer CookieContainer = new
CookieContainer();

        protected override WebRequest GetWebRequest(Uri address)
        {
            var request = base.GetWebRequest(address);
            if (request is HttpWebRequest)
                ((HttpWebRequest)request).CookieContainer =
CookieContainer;
            return request;
        }
    }
}
```

Binding helper

In WPF, the input element for passwords does not provide binding for the actual content of it. This is due to security reasons. It has been made hard to get passwords and bind these to something such as a ViewModel that will potentially keep the string in an insecure manner and then provide a security hole. However, we will violate this by creating a little helper that will make it possible for us to bind it back to a ViewModel. An improvement to this, which could fly better in a real-world scenario, would be to make it explicitly only support SecureString that the .NET Framework supports.

Add a file called PasswordHelper in the root of the project. Make the class look as follows:

```
using System.Reflection;
using System.Security;
using System.Windows;
using System.Windows.Controls;
using System.Windows.Data;

namespace SignalRChat.WPF
{
    public class PasswordHelper
    {
        public static DependencyProperty
BindablePasswordEnabledProperty =
            DependencyProperty.RegisterAttached(
                "BindablePasswordEnabled",
                typeof(bool),
                typeof(PasswordHelper),
                new PropertyMetadata(BindablePasswordEnabledChanged));

        private static void BindablePasswordEnabledChanged(DependencyO
bject d, DependencyPropertyChangedEventArgs e)
        {
            var passwordBox = d as PasswordBox;
            passwordBox.PasswordChanged += (s, ee) =>
            {
                var password = passwordBox.Password;
```

```
                BindingExpression bindingExpression
= BindingOperations.GetBindingExpression(passwordBox,
BindablePasswordProperty);
                if (bindingExpression != null)
                {
                    PropertyInfo property = bindingExpression.
DataItem.GetType().GetProperty(bindingExpression.ParentBinding.Path.
Path);
                    if (property != null)
                        property.SetValue(bindingExpression.DataItem,
password, null);
                }
            };
        }


        public static bool GetBindablePasswordEnabled(PasswordBox
passwordBox)
        {
            return (bool)passwordBox.GetValue(BindablePasswordEnabled
Property);
        }


        public static void SetBindablePasswordEnabled(PasswordBox
passwordBox, bool enabled)
        {
            passwordBox.SetValue(BindablePasswordEnabledProperty,
enabled);
        }


        public static DependencyProperty BindablePasswordProperty =
            DependencyProperty.RegisterAttached(
                "BindablePassword",
                typeof(string),
                typeof(PasswordHelper));


        public static string GetBindablePassword(PasswordBox
passwordBox)
        {
            return passwordBox.Password;
        }
```

```
        public static void SetBindablePassword(PasswordBox
passwordBox, string password)
        {
            passwordBox.Password = password;
        }
    }
}
```

Basically, the code puts in place a couple of attached dependency properties that makes it possible for us to bind the password property back to anything through bindings.

Creating a client security service

The last piece of the infrastructure puzzle that we will need before starting on the actual UI is the thing that connects to the server and actually performs the authentication. We will build a service that is represented with an interface, making it possible for us to swap implementations and also making it possible for us to write automated unit tests that only test the unit having the security system as a dependency, without having to have the concrete type. Basically, with this, we can provide any fake or mock implementation and test that the interaction is correct. We won't go into the topic of testing in this book, but keep in mind that, with this type of decoupling, there is a great opportunity to write simpler tests that enables you to put things in higher isolation without having to set up a full environment for every test. We will represent our authentication mechanism through an interface:

1. Add an interface called ISecurity at the root of the project.
2. Make it look as follows:

```
using System.Net;

namespace SignalRChat.WPF
{
    public interface ISecurity
    {
        CookieContainer CookieContainer { get; }

        bool Authenticate(string userName, string password);
    }
}
```

3. With the interface in place, we want to create an implementation that will automatically be hooked up by Bifrosts built-in convention to match interfaces to the classes in the `IFoo` to `Foo` convention. Add a class called `Security` to the root of the project. Make the class look as follows:

```
using System.Collections.Specialized;
using System.Net;
using Bifrost.Execution;

namespace SignalRChat.WPF
{
    [Singleton]
    public class Security : ISecurity
    {
        const string Site = "http://localhost:3705";

        public CookieContainer CookieContainer { get; private set; }

        public bool Authenticate(string userName, string password)
        {
            var postData = new NameValueCollection();
            postData.Add("userName", userName);
            postData.Add("password", password);

            var url = string.Format("{0}/SecurityHandler.ashx",
Site);
            var webClient = new CookieAwareWebClient();
            try
            {
                webClient.UploadValues(url, postData);
            }
            catch (WebException)
            {
                return false;
            }
            CookieContainer = webClient.CookieContainer;
            return true;
        }
    }
}
```

Notice the [Singleton] attribute. Bifrost uses this information during its hookup and identifies the implementation as something that should only be one instance of, and will, therefore, register it with the IoC container with such a life cycle.

Another important aspect is that the constant called site must match the URL and port number of the actual website.

Adding a login view

With the infrastructure in place, we can start putting in place the UI for logging in:

1. We will divide the different features into user controls. Add a user control called Login.xaml by right-clicking on the project and navigating to **Add | New Item**. In the **Add New Item** dialog box, select **User Control (WPF)** and give it the name Login.xaml. Then, click on the **Add** button:

2. In the **Xaml** view, you can edit things, which will be a lot easier than going through the **Design** view. Let's add the following XML namespace declaration on the UserControl element:

```
xmlns:viewModels="clr-namespace:Bifrost.
ViewModels;assembly=Bifrost.Client"
xmlns:interaction="clr-namespace:Bifrost.
Interaction;assembly=Bifrost.Client"
xmlns:local="clr-namespace:SignalRChat.WPF"
```

3. On the `UserControl` element, we now want to hook up the ViewModel, which we will create later. Add the following attribute to the element:

```
DataContext="{viewModels:ViewModel {x:Type local:LoginViewModel}}"
```

 The ViewModel markup extension in Bifrost will take the type given as parameter and use the IoC container to create an instance when it's needed. This results in the dependencies that the ViewModel might have to be resolved.

4. Now, we are going to need the actual UI with typically a `UserName`, `Password`, and a button for logging in. Within the `Grid` element in the XAML, add the following:

```
<StackPanel Orientation="Vertical" Margin="8">
    <Label>UserName</Label>
    <TextBox Text="{Binding UserName}"></TextBox>
    <Label>Password</Label>
    <PasswordBox x:Name="password"
                        local:PasswordHelper.
BindablePasswordEnabled="true"
                        local:PasswordHelper.
BindablePassword="{Binding Password}"
                        />
    <Button Command="{interaction:FromMethod SignIn}">Sign in</
Button>
</StackPanel>
```

 Notice the usage of the `PasswordHelper`, we're telling it first to enable the binding of the password and then the binding for the password.

The `FromMethod` extension is something Bifrost provides to enable a declarative way of binding a method on ViewModel as an `ICommand`, which covers most of the scenarios. The markup extension has more support as well, such as the `CanExecuteWhen` property that can point to a property that can tell whether or not execution can happen; if it's sitting on a type implementing `INotifyPropertyChanged`, it will respond to change.

5. Now, we need the ViewModel. The ViewModel will need to be able to take the `UserName` and `Password` and then provide a method for doing the `SignIn`. Add a class called `LoginViewModel` to the root of the project.

6. Add the following statement at the top:

```
using PropertyChanged;
```

7. From the `PropertyChanged` namespace, we get access to an attribute that we will adorn our ViewModel with:

```
[ImplementPropertyChanged]
public class LoginViewModel
{
}
```

 With this, we're telling a post-build task to implement the `INotifyPropertyChanged` interface for the class and to make all public properties notify for changes when they get set with values.

8. For the View to not have any exceptions, we will have to add some properties and a behavior for actually logging into the system. Add the following code to the ViewModel:

```
public string UserName { get; set; }
public string Password { get; set; }

public void SignIn()
{
}
```

9. Now, we have the scaffolding that makes the View work. Let's move on to the actual signing in. The ViewModel will delegate this work to other systems — especially the security system that we created. Therefore, we will need a dependency for it. We will also need a dependency for a messenger. Add the following statement at the top of the file:

```
using Bifrost.Messaging;
```

10. Then, we're ready to add the following private fields and constructor to the ViewModel:

```
IMessenger _messenger;
ISecurity _security;

public LoginViewModel(IMessenger messenger, ISecurity security)
{
    _messenger = messenger;
    _security = security;
}
```

Ninject, as the IoC container, will resolve the dependencies given in the form of constructor parameters. With this approach, we get an opportunity to write automated tests for the ViewModel without having to test anything specific in the dependencies, but make sure the ViewModel interacts correctly with them. The messenger is something we will use to broadcast when we're logged in without coupling ViewModels together.

11. Let's go ahead and create a message that we will broadcast when we're logged in. Add a class to the root of the project called `LoggedIn`. Just leave it as is; we will not need anything more.

12. Now, we will expand on the `SignIn()` method in the ViewModel. Let's sign in and, if successful, broadcast that we are logged in. Make the `SignIn()` method look as follows:

```
public void SignIn()
{
    if (_security.Authenticate(UserName, Password))
    {
        _messenger.Publish(new LoggedIn());
    }
}
```

The hub proxy

After we're logged in, we can start thinking about SignalR and consuming the hub that we have on the server. The proxy generation we have with JavaScript for the web solution is not available for .NET clients. In order to keep with the theme of decoupling and making our code testable, we want to introduce a proxy and define it through an interface representing the functionality that we will consume and then create a concrete implementation that will work with the SignalR client APIs.

Add an interface called `IChatHub` to the root of the project and make it look as follows:

```
using System;
using Microsoft.AspNet.SignalR.Client;

namespace SignalRChat.WPF
{
    public interface IChatHub
    {
```

```
        event Action<StateChange> StateChanged;
        event Action<string> JoinedRoom;
        event Action<string> RoomAdded;
        event Action<string> MessageReceived;

        string CurrentChatRoom { get; }
        void Join(string room);
        void CreateRoom(string room);
        void Send(string message);
    }
}
```

Then, we can implement this interface. Add a class called ChatHub representing the implementation of the interface we just defined, to the root of the project.

1. Make the class implement the IChatHub interface and mark the class as singleton; we only want one instance of this in memory at any given time:

```
[Singleton]
public class ChatHub : IChatHub
{
}
```

2. From the IChatHub interface, let's implement the events at the top of the class:

```
public event Action<StateChange> StateChanged = (state) => { };
public event Action<string> JoinedRoom = (room) => { };
public event Action<string> RoomAdded = (room) => { };
public event Action<string> MessageReceived = (message) => { };
```

 The lambda expression makes the event have a default event handler, the lambda expression makes the event have a default event handler. This lets any code ignore checking for null before calling the event. In my opinion, null is inherently bad, making code more complex than it needs to be. It's easy to avoid having null to be a valid state for anything.

3. Let's add a couple of private fields and a constructor that takes the dependencies we will need:

```
ISecurity _security;
IHubProxy _chatProxy;
```

```
public ChatHub(IMessenger messenger, ISecurity security)
{
    _security = security;
    messenger.SubscribeTo<LoggedIn>(LoggedIn);
}
```

4. The last line suggests a method called LoggedIn to be called on ChatHub whenever we receive the LoggedIn message. Since we choose to just publish a LoggedIn message, anyone can subscribe to it in our system. When we're logged in, we want to create the connection to the hub. Let's add a private variable to the ChatHub class:

```
HubConnection _hubConnection;
```

5. We will also need a constant to hold information about the URL to connect to. Add this at the top of the class and make sure it matches your site's URL and port number:

```
const string Site = "http://localhost:3705";
```

6. Now, let's implement the LoggedIn method:

```
void LoggedIn(LoggedIn loggedIn)
{
    _hubConnection = new HubConnection(Site);
    _hubConnection.CookieContainer = _security.CookieContainer;
    _hubConnection.StateChanged += (s) => StateChanged(s);

    _chatProxy = _hubConnection.CreateHubProxy("chat");
    _chatProxy.On("addMessage", (string message) =>
MessageReceived(message));
    _chatProxy.On("addChatRoom", (string room) =>
RoomAdded(room));

    CurrentChatRoom = "Lobby";
    JoinedRoom(CurrentChatRoom);

    _hubConnection.Start().Wait();
}
```

Since we expose the container of cookies from the security system, we can use this directly on the connection. From HubConnection, we can create the actual underlying proxy object that we will be working with for communication.

To handle any messages sent from the server, we use the .On() method on the underlying proxy and specify the client message and handler. In our particular case, we've gone for an inline lambda, but we could easily have just a private method on this particular class.

7. With the hub connection in place, we can implement the rest of the IChatHub interface, making our proxy come alive:

```
public void Join(string room)
{
    _chatProxy.Invoke("Join", room).Wait();
    JoinedRoom(room);
}

public void CreateRoom(string room)
{
    _chatProxy.Invoke("CreateChatRoom", room).Wait();
    JoinedRoom(room);
}

public void Send(string message)
{
    _chatProxy.Invoke("Send", message);
}

public string CurrentChatRoom
{
    get { return (string)_chatProxy["currentChatRoom"]; }
    private set { _chatProxy["currentChatRoom"] = value; }
}
```

Note that, when calling hubs on the server, it's basically just
.Invoke() on the proxy representation. The second parameter is in
fact a params collection, so you can give it any parameters and these
will be sent along to match the signature on the server.

Lastly is the state that gets carried around for each round trip to the
server; the proxy exposes an indexer enabling us to set any state as if it
is a dictionary.

Our chat rooms

With the login in place and knowing the secret behind how to actually do
the SignalR bits and pieces in a .NET client, we want to rush to the conclusion.
Let's quickly run through the last bits as we need to start with the feature that will
list chat rooms and allow the user to select a room to chat in.

As before, add another `UserControl`; this time, let's call it `ChatRooms`. Make the
XAML look as follows:

```
<UserControl x:Class="SignalRChat.WPF.ChatRooms"
             xmlns="http://schemas.microsoft.com/winfx/2006/xaml/
presentation"
             xmlns:x="http://schemas.microsoft.com/winfx/2006/xaml"
             xmlns:mc="http://schemas.openxmlformats.org/markup-
compatibility/2006"
             xmlns:d="http://schemas.microsoft.com/expression/
blend/2008"
             xmlns:viewModels="clr-namespace:Bifrost.
ViewModels;assembly=Bifrost.Client"
             xmlns:interaction="clr-namespace:Bifrost.
Interaction;assembly=Bifrost.Client"
             xmlns:local="clr-namespace:SignalRChat.WPF"
             mc:Ignorable="d"
             d:DesignHeight="300" d:DesignWidth="300"
             DataContext="{viewModels:ViewModel {x:Type
local:ChatRoomsViewModel}}"
             >
    <Grid>
        <Grid.RowDefinitions>
            <RowDefinition Height="*"/>
            <RowDefinition Height="30"/>
        </Grid.RowDefinitions>
```

```
<Grid Grid.Row="0" VerticalAlignment="Stretch" Height="Auto">
    <Grid.RowDefinitions>
        <RowDefinition Height="30"/>
        <RowDefinition Height="*"/>
    </Grid.RowDefinitions>
    <Label Grid.Row="0">Chatroom</Label>
    <ListView Grid.Row="1"
            ItemsSource="{Binding Rooms}"
            SelectedItem="{Binding CurrentRoom}">
    </ListView>
</Grid>

<Grid Grid.Row="1">
    <Grid.ColumnDefinitions>
        <ColumnDefinition Width="*"/>
        <ColumnDefinition Width="100"/>
    </Grid.ColumnDefinitions>

    <TextBox Grid.Column="0" x:Name="room"/>
    <Button Grid.Column="1"
            Command="{interaction:FromMethod AddRoom}"
            CommandParameter="{Binding ElementName=room,
Path=Text}">
        Create room
    </Button>
</Grid>
    </Grid>
</UserControl>
```

We are pretty much doing the same things as before. We have a listing of rooms, and the selected room gets bound back to a property on the upcoming ViewModel called `CurrentRoom`. The button for adding a room has a binding for `CommandParameter` to get the actual text directly from the `TextBox` element. This approach allows us to keep the view concern in the view and not introduce variables that are really not needed on the ViewModel. With this in place, let's add the ViewModel for it. Add a class called `ChatRoomsViewModel` in the root of the project. Make it look as follows:

```
using System;
using System.Collections.ObjectModel;
using System.Windows;
using PropertyChanged;
```

```
namespace SignalRChat.WPF
{
    [ImplementPropertyChanged]
    public class ChatRoomsViewModel
    {
        IChatHub _chatHub;
        string _currentRoom;

        public ChatRoomsViewModel(IChatHub chatHub)
        {
            _chatHub = chatHub;
            _currentRoom = "Lobby";

            Rooms = new ObservableCollection<string>();

            chatHub.RoomAdded += (room) => Application.Current.
Dispatcher.BeginInvoke((Action)(() => Rooms.Add(room)));
        }

        public ObservableCollection<string> Rooms { get; private set;
}

        public string CurrentRoom
        {
            get { return _currentRoom; }
            set
            {
                _currentRoom = value;
                _chatHub.Join(value);
            }
        }

        public void AddRoom(string room)
        {
            _chatHub.CreateRoom(room);
        }
    }
}
```

As you can see, we're now consuming the hub, taking it in as a dependency on the constructor; again, making it easier for us to test the interaction with it. For the `RoomAdded` event handler, we have to use `dispatcher` to make sure we add items to the UI thread. In my opinion, this is a leaky abstraction and something I'd expect `ObservableCollection` to take care of, as the ViewModel has no interest in knowing about anything related to the View, not even knowing whether there is a view at all. However, enough about this. All the interaction is done directly against the `IChatHub` interface, and our ViewModel is again just delegating the work, which is its job.

The chat

Let's keep the same pace for the final feature. Add a new `UserControl` called `Chat` in the root of the project, and make it look as follows:

```
<UserControl x:Class="SignalRChat.WPF.Chat"
             xmlns="http://schemas.microsoft.com/winfx/2006/xaml/
presentation"
             xmlns:x="http://schemas.microsoft.com/winfx/2006/xaml"
             xmlns:mc="http://schemas.openxmlformats.org/markup-
compatibility/2006"
             xmlns:d="http://schemas.microsoft.com/expression/
blend/2008"
             xmlns:viewModels="clr-namespace:Bifrost.
ViewModels;assembly=Bifrost.Client"
             xmlns:interaction="clr-namespace:Bifrost.
Interaction;assembly=Bifrost.Client"
             xmlns:local="clr-namespace:SignalRChat.WPF"
             mc:Ignorable="d"
             d:DesignHeight="300" d:DesignWidth="300"
             DataContext="{viewModels:ViewModel {x:Type
local:ChatViewModel}}">
    <Grid>
        <Grid.RowDefinitions>
            <RowDefinition Height="*"/>
            <RowDefinition Height="30"/>
        </Grid.RowDefinitions>

        <Grid Grid.Row="0" VerticalAlignment="Stretch" Height="Auto">
            <Grid.RowDefinitions>
                <RowDefinition Height="30"/>
```

```xml
                            <RowDefinition Height="*"/>
                        </Grid.RowDefinitions>
                        <TextBlock>
                            <Run>Current Room : </Run>
                            <Run Text="{Binding CurrentRoom, Mode=OneWay}"/>
                            <Run>, Current State : </Run>
                            <Run Text="{Binding CurrentState, Mode=OneWay}"/>
                        </TextBlock>
                        <ListView Grid.Row="1" ItemsSource="{Binding Messages}"></
ListView>
                    </Grid>
                    <Grid Grid.Row="1">
                        <Grid.ColumnDefinitions>
                            <ColumnDefinition Width="*"/>
                            <ColumnDefinition Width="150"/>
                        </Grid.ColumnDefinitions>

                        <TextBox Grid.Column="0" x:Name="message"/>
                        <Button Grid.Column="1"
                                Command="{interaction:FromMethod Send}"
                                CommandParameter="{Binding ElementName=message,
Path=Text}">Send</Button>
                    </Grid>
            </Grid>
    </UserControl>
```

There is nothing much to add about this feature; it's just repeating the same kind of concepts that we've already done previously. Now, jump to creating the ViewModel for the view. Add a class called ChatViewModel to the root of the project, and make it look as follows:

```csharp
using System;
using System.Collections.ObjectModel;
using System.Windows;
using PropertyChanged;

namespace SignalRChat.WPF
{
    [ImplementPropertyChanged]
    public class ChatViewModel
    {
        IChatHub _chatHub;
```

```
        public ChatViewModel(IChatHub chatHub)
        {
            _chatHub = chatHub;
            CurrentState = "Disconnected";

            Messages = new ObservableCollection<string>();

            chatHub.StateChanged += (stateChange) => CurrentState =
stateChange.NewState.ToString();
            chatHub.JoinedRoom += (room) =>
            {
                Application.Current.Dispatcher.BeginInvoke((Action)(()
=>
                {
                    CurrentRoom = room;
                    Messages.Clear();
                    Messages.Add("Joined : " + room);
                }));
            };

            chatHub.MessageReceived += (message) => Application.
Current.Dispatcher.BeginInvoke((Action)(() => Messages.Add(message)));
        }

        public string CurrentRoom { get; private set; }
        public string CurrentState { get; private set; }

        public ObservableCollection<string> Messages { get; private
set; }

        public void Send(string message)
        {
            _chatHub.Send(message);
        }
    }
}
```

This concludes the features. We're now ready to get our feature visible in the application.

The composition

Now that we have all that in place, we will still not be able to see anything on the screen if we run the application. We will need to bring this all into `MainWindow` that was created for us when we created the project.

Make the `MainWindow.xaml` file look as follows:

```xml
<Window x:Class="SignalRChat.WPF.MainWindow"
        xmlns="http://schemas.microsoft.com/winfx/2006/xaml/
presentation"
        xmlns:x="http://schemas.microsoft.com/winfx/2006/xaml"
        xmlns:local="clr-namespace:SignalRChat.WPF"
        xmlns:viewModels="clr-namespace:Bifrost.
ViewModels;assembly=Bifrost.Client"
        xmlns:interaction="clr-namespace:Bifrost.
Interaction;assembly=Bifrost.Client"
        Title="MainWindow"
        Height="400"
        Width="600"
        DataContext="{viewModels:ViewModel {x:Type
local:MainWindowViewModel}}">
    <Grid Margin="8">
        <Grid.Resources>
            <local:BooleanToVisibilityConverter x:Key="BooleanToVisibi
lityConverter"/>
        </Grid.Resources>

        <Grid Visibility="{Binding LoggedIn, Converter={StaticResource
BooleanToVisibilityConverter}}">
            <Grid.ColumnDefinitions>
                <ColumnDefinition Width="250"/>
                <ColumnDefinition Width="*"/>
            </Grid.ColumnDefinitions>

            <local:ChatRooms Grid.Column="0"/>
            <local:Chat Grid.Column="1"/>
        </Grid>

        <Grid Visibility="{Binding LoggedIn, Converter={StaticResource
BooleanToVisibilityConverter}, ConverterParameter=true}">
            <local:Login/>
        </Grid>
    </Grid>
</Window>
```

Note that we made the window a bit larger than the default. Also, we're introducing the usage of a value converter. Value converters are valuable in converting values, often between different types. In our case, we will have a `boolean` on the ViewModel, but it will need to be converted to a certain `Visibility` type, to do this we use the `BooleanToVisibilityConverter`. The purpose of this, as you can see in the grids surrounding the different features, is to turn on and off the visibility of the different features depending on whether or not we're logged in. If you're familiar with WPF development, you might be asking yourself why are we not using the built-in converter that has the same name. The answer is that we have a second requirement: we want it to be able to take a Boolean in and flip the result so that we can have one boolean used for two scenarios. Notice the converter parameter that will tell it to negate the result or not of the boolean. Add a class called `BooleanToVisibilityConverter` in the root of the project. Make the class look as follows:

```
using System;
using System.Globalization;
using System.Windows;
using System.Windows.Data;

namespace SignalRChat.WPF
{
    public class BooleanToVisibilityConverter : IValueConverter
    {
        public object Convert(object value, Type targetType, object parameter, CultureInfo culture)
        {
            var visible = (bool)value;
            if (parameter != null && bool.Parse(parameter.ToString())
== true) visible ^= true;
            return visible ? Visibility.Visible : Visibility.Hidden;
        }

        public object ConvertBack(object value, Type targetType,
object parameter, CultureInfo culture)
        {
            throw new System.NotImplementedException();
        }
    }
}
```

We're only interested in converting one way, but it could have been supporting going back as well. The converter supports a parameter that can be `true` or `false`, indicating whether or not to flip the meaning of the `boolean` value coming in.

Now, we can go ahead and create the ViewModel for `MainWindow`. Add a class called `MainWindowViewModel` to the root of the project:

```
using Bifrost.Messaging;
using PropertyChanged;

namespace SignalRChat.WPF
{
    [ImplementPropertyChanged]
    public class MainWindowViewModel
    {
        public MainWindowViewModel(IMessenger messenger)
        {
            messenger.SubscribeTo<LoggedIn>(m => LoggedIn = true);
        }

        public bool LoggedIn { get; private set; }
    }
}
```

As you can see here, we have the second use of consuming the `LoggedIn` message without having to alter the publisher. This proves how we can scale a system without all the parts knowing about each other.

If we've done everything right and our website is running, launching the app should yield a login window, as shown here:

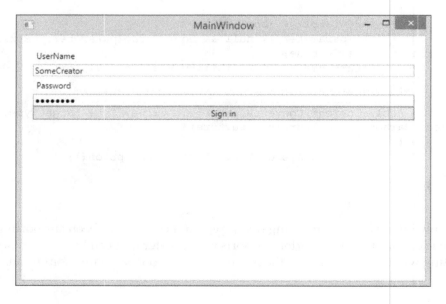

Logging in should yield the following window:

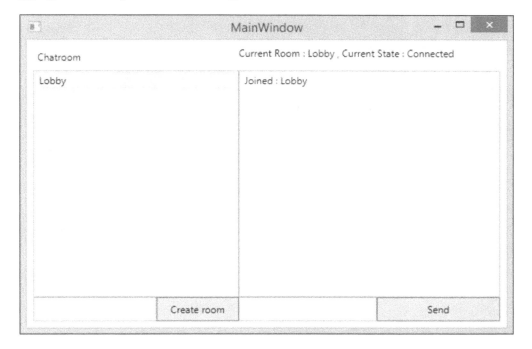

Summary

Although there are differences between creating a web solution and a desktop client, the differences have faded over time. We can apply the same principles across the different environments; it's just different programming languages. The SignalR API adds the same type of consistency in thinking, although not as matured as the JavaScript API with proxy generation and so on; still the same ideas and concepts are found in the underlying API. Creating the proxies ourselves is not all that much work either. We've seen how easy it is to consume the same hub used in the web solution on a .NET client.

In the next chapter, we're going to see how we can use this knowledge and approach to build something that moves across the boundaries of three more platforms in the mobile space.

Write Once, Deploy Many
9

In this chapter, we will create a mobile experience covering the full feature set from the web client and the WPF client. The goal is to enable us to bring this feature set to all the major mobile clients out there—iOS, Android, and Windows Phone—but without having to rewrite it for every platform natively. The following topics will be covered in this chapter:

- Understanding Xamarin
- Getting an environment up and running for iOS development using a Mac
- Utilizing Visual Studio from a Virtual Machine on the Mac, and connecting directly to the device simulator and a real device
- Getting an environment up and running for Android
- MVVM and XAML
- How to consume Hubs
- How to work with groups

Cross platform

Ever since the release of Microsoft .NET 1.0 back in 2002, it has grown to more and more platforms, not only on Microsoft's own platforms but also others. Already in 2003, we saw an open source implementation for BSD variants called **DotGNU** and its Portable .NET. In 2004, the initial release of Mono came out, whereas a second open source implementation aimed at Linux and Mac OS X. All of a sudden in 2007 with Silverlight, we saw Microsoft targeting multiple platforms themselves with Windows and Mac OS X with an implementation of the CLR and a subset of .NET Framework.

Over the years, we've seen Silverlight come and go, and then Windows Phone 7 came along, which kind of picked up Silverlight and brought it in the future. Back in 2006, before Silverlight came, Microsoft launched **Windows Presentation Foundation (WPF)** — a new way to perform client development on the Windows stack. This is what Silverlight was built around; a subset of and also what Windows Phone 7 brought with it further as well. With Windows 8 and the store applications, Microsoft invested even more in XAML, but again for a new implementation. The people behind Mono did implement a Silverlight version to run on Linux, as Microsoft only provided OS X, which was called **Moonlight**. It never quite matured before being abandoned and was sitting in a hybrid state of supporting some of the features in Silverlight version 1 and some of version 2 and 3, even some of version 4 sneaking in.

Xamarin is a company that is leading the development of Mono. The company provides professional services for Mono and also branded editions of the IDE used for Mono called **MonoDevelop** (its branded version is called **Xamarin Studio**). Fast forwarding to 2014, Xamarin launched something called as Xamarin Forms: a set of commercial tools to rapidly build mobile applications, targeting the most popular mobile platforms out there with a *write once, run many* philosophy. Xamarin Forms is yet another XAML dialect, not as fully matured as the ones found in Microsoft, but nevertheless really powerful and fully capable of delivering very rich applications. It's already built on top of Xamarin's **MonoTouch** and **MonoDroid**, which are the .NET binding implementations for iOS and Android.

Obviously, there are multiple choices out there for going cross-platform with a single codebase. There are things such as Cordova, Ionic, and many more. Xamarin is a commercial product targeting the .NET space, which is basically why I chose to put it in here instead of other options.

Getting started

Before you start, you might want to run down to your local Apple Store and pick up a Mac, if you haven't already got one. Just kidding! The code is the same no matter which platform you choose, but as the iOS one is the hardest with most moving parts, we'll focus on this. In fact, this is a lot cheaper than buying a Mac. There are, in fact, cloud providers that will give you a virtual Mac in the cloud (for instance, the commercial provider: `http://www.macincloud.com`). The reason you need a Mac is because of the way Xamarin actually gets compiled. When you're writing code in C#, it will not run inside a runtime on iOS, but it will be compiled down to a native language for iOS.

In order for Xamarin to be able to do this, it relies on tools found in Xcode, which is only available on Mac. The same approach is for Android. It does not have a **Common Language Runtime (CLR)**. So, it compiles down to what is right for Android and runs it. Any references you have will be included, but it's really smart and does not include things you're not using. Therefore, if you have a reference to an assembly from the base class library, it will extract the functionality that is used and natively compiles it down and only includes this. This way, you don't have a full copy of the .NET Framework embedded in your application on the devices but only the stuff your application consists of. When you install Xamarin, it will download the necessary prerequisites too. So, if you install it on Mac, it will download whatever it needs to be able to do the things it needs. Likewise for Android; it will download the environment and emulators so that you can get started. Microsoft has also built an emulator themselves for Android that integrates even better in Visual Studio for a better developer experience. When doing this, read more about it at `http://blogs.msdn.com/b/visualstudioalm/archive/2014/11/12/introducing-visual-studio-s-emulator-for-android.aspx`.

I am a Mac user myself and my setup consists of OS X as my host operating system and then I run Windows in a virtualized environment; I prefer using parallels for virtualization. In order for us to get things working, you will have to switch from Shared Networking to Bridged Networking, as we will access the virtual computer through its IP address.

Once your OS X environment is good to go, you will need software (this is where it might sting a bit). Xamarin Forms is not free and the cheapest you can get is the Indie license. Once you've decided which way to go with licensing, you will need the software, which can all be found at `http://xamarin.com/forms`. You have the option of working with Visual Studio or Xamarin Studio. I've chosen to use Visual Studio, as everything in this book, so far, has been based on it. In addition to this, you will have to get Xcode installed on your OS X host. This can be done through the OS X app store. In addition, you'll have to read the documentation from Xamarin to see how to connect your Visual Studio to Xcode through its build host, as this book can't cover the entire environment setup.

A slight health warning: there are typically things you'd need to do such as keep configuration in a clever way and also deal with errors that can occur. The code in this chapter is naive in this way. Anyway, let's get started:

1. Inside Visual Studio, we want to add a new project to the solution. Right-click on the solution in **Solution Explorer** and select **Add | New Project**.

2. From the left-hand side menu, select **Mobile Apps** and then select **Blank App (Xamarin.Forms Portable)**:

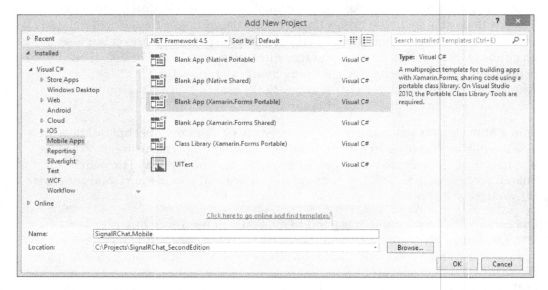

You should now have four new projects: **SignalRChat.Mobile.Droid**, **SignalRChat. Mobile.WinPhone**, **SignalRChat.Mobile.iOS**, and **SignalRChat.Mobile**. The last project is where we are going to do the majority of the work proving that we can write most of our code once and still get it to work on multiple platforms. This particular walk-through, however, will focus on getting the iOS stuff working, as it is the most complex setup with two machines involved + an emulator hosted on the Mac side of things.

The other two platforms should be fairly simple to get running by just setting the projects to start up and running them:

1. Let's set the iOS project as the startup project by right-clicking on the project and selecting **Set as StartUp Project**:

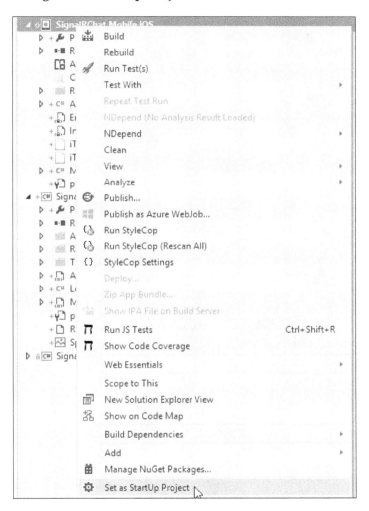

2. In the standard toolbox in Visual Studio, you should also now have a drop-down list to select which iPhone to target. You can certainly choose whatever feels right for you, but throughout this walk-through, we're using the iPhone 4s, which would give you the largest reach.

3. At the time of writing this book there are a few minor issues with Xamarin; one of them being that it won't necessarily build all projects as it should. This can cause a lot of head-scratching when you're changing things in the common project and it is not being reflected in the running code. This is easy to fix; right-click on the solution in **Solution Explorer** and select **Configuration Manager...**:

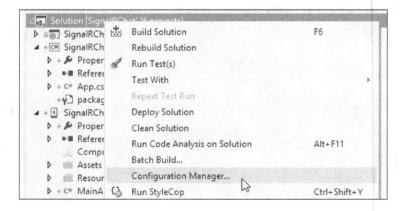

4. In the **Configuration Manager...**, we want to make sure both the iOS project and the common project is set to **Build**. Check the checkbox the **SignalRChat.Mobile** project if it is not already checked:

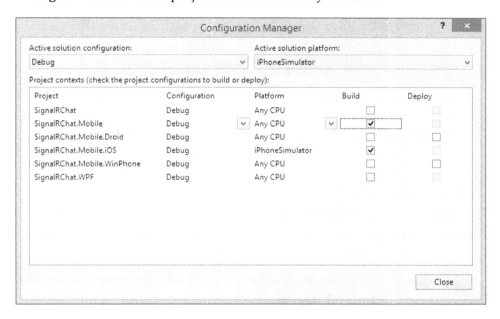

Code signing

If you are not a registered Apple developer, but are just using Xamarin and eventually Xcode without yet thinking about going to the store, you won't have the necessary certificates on the OS X side to actually sign the binaries. You will quickly run into compiler errors telling you that your application can't be signed.

This is fairly simple to fix; all we need to do is manually edit the project file:

1. Unload the iOS project from **Solution Explorer**:

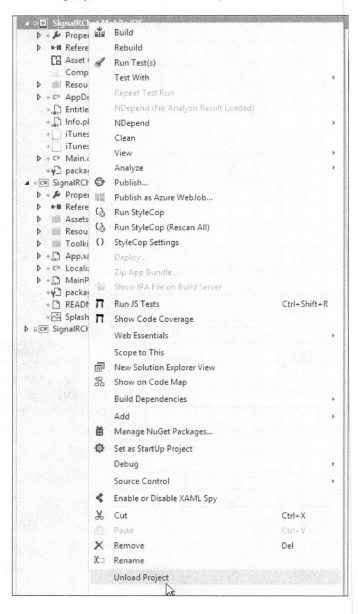

2. Right-click on the unloaded project and choose to edit it:

3. For instance, in the Debug configuration, we want to remove the file reference in something called CodesignEntitlements:

```
<PropertyGroup Condition=" '$(Configuration)|$(Platform)' == 'Debug|iPhoneSimulator' ">
  <DebugSymbols>true</DebugSymbols>
  <DebugType>full</DebugType>
  <Optimize>false</Optimize>
  <OutputPath>bin\iPhoneSimulator\Debug</OutputPath>
  <DefineConstants>DEBUG</DefineConstants>
  <ErrorReport>prompt</ErrorReport>
  <WarningLevel>4</WarningLevel>
  <ConsolePause>false</ConsolePause>
  <MtouchArch>i386, x86_64</MtouchArch>
  <MtouchLink>None</MtouchLink>
  <MtouchDebug>true</MtouchDebug>
  <CodesignEntitlements>Entitlements.plist</CodesignEntitlements>
</PropertyGroup>
```

4. Now, we can reload the project by right-clicking on it and selecting the **Reload Project** action:

With the build host running on the OS X side of things and Visual Studio that is paired with it, as described in the Xamarin documentation, you should now be able to run the project using *Ctrl + F5* (**Debug | Run without debugger**). It should yield the following result in the emulator:

Preparing for connections

In order for us to be able to connect from OSX to SignalR, we're going to have to do some changes to the **IIS Express** configuration:

1. Locate the **IIS Express** icon in the **system tray**:

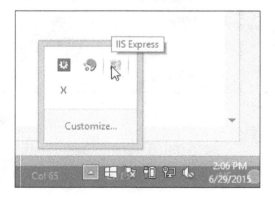

2. Right-click on it and select **Show All Applications**:

3. From the dialog box, select the site for the application and look at the path of the configuration file. Make a note of this as we're going to need it real soon:

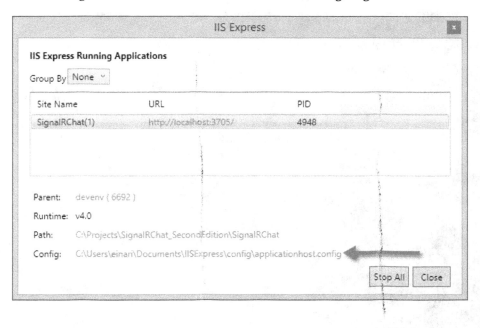

4. We want to stop the site, since we're changing its configuration. Right-click on the tray icon to locate IIS Express again and select **Stop Site**:

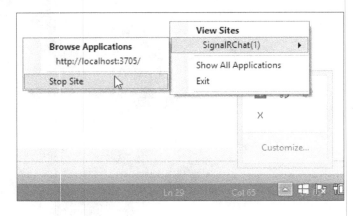

5. We need to know the IP address of the Windows computer that is hosting the website. One way of doing this is to open up a console/cmd and just type `ipconfig`; make note of **IPv4 Address**:

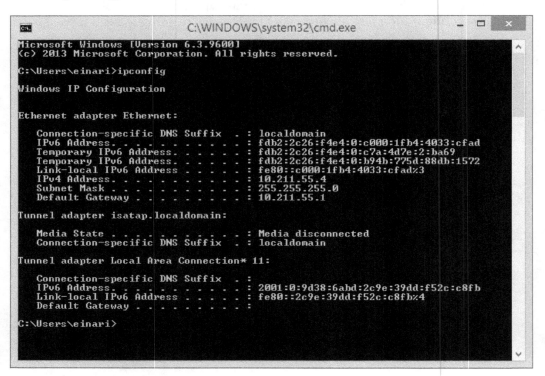

6. Open the config file from the path we found in the IIS Express configuration, using something such as Notepad or whatever your favorite text editor is. Inside it, search for the `<site>` tag. Under the `<bindings>` tag, we want to add a binding other than `localhost`, with the specific IP address that we found. Copy and paste the `localhost` line and swap out `localhost` in the pasted line with the IP address:

```
<site name="SignalRChat" id="40">
    <application path="/" applicationPool="Clr4IntegratedAppPool">
        <virtualDirectory path="/" physicalPath="C:\Projects\SignalRChat_SecondEdition\SignalRChat" />
    </application>
    <bindings>
        <binding protocol="http" bindingInformation="*:3705:localhost" />
        <binding protocol="http" bindingInformation="*:3705:10.211.55.4" />
    </bindings>
</site>
```

If you have the firewall enabled in Windows, now would be a good time to add a TCP port exception for the port; in my case, it is `3705`.

Packages

We are going to need some packages. The packages will only need to be added to the common project: **SignalRChat.Mobile**. First, let's add a reference to SignalR by adding the package called `Microsoft.AspNet.SignalR.Client`. After this, add a reference to `SimpleInjector`, a simple IoC container implementation. We could have used Ninject or others here as well. There are, however, some limitations with some of the magic that was going on when we used Ninject together with Bifrost that is yet to be solved by these libraries; therefore, we just use this for simplicity instead.

MVVM

In *Chapter 8, Building a WPF .NET Client*, we had some help for doing MVVM from a package called **Bifrost**. This package does not yet support Xamarin, so we are going to borrow some of the concepts from it, although a bit more naïvely implemented. I would recommend taking a look at the source code for Bifrost (`http://github.com/dolittle/bifrost`), for a fully featured version. For now, however, it will do.

Messenger

The publish/subscribe mechanism we have is fairly simple to implement.
Let's add the interface that represents the functionality we need:

1. Add an interface called `IMessenger` in the common **SignalRChat.Mobile** project.

2. Make the interface look as follows:

```
public interface IMessenger
{
    void Publish<T>(T content);
    void SubscribeTo<T>(Action<T> receivedCallback);
}
```

3. We will need an implementation for the interface; add a class called `Messenger` sitting in the same project. Make the class look as follows:

```
public class Messenger : IMessenger
{
    Dictionary<Type, List<Delegate>> _subscribers = new
Dictionary<Type, List<Delegate>>();

    public void Publish<T>(T content)
    {
        var type = typeof(T);
        if (_subscribers.ContainsKey(type))
        {
            foreach (var subscriber in _subscribers[type])
            {
                subscriber.DynamicInvoke(content);
            }
        }
    }

    public void SubscribeTo<T>(Action<T> receivedCallback)
    {
        var type = typeof(T);
        List<Delegate> subscribersList = null;
        if (_subscribers.ContainsKey(type))
            subscribersList = _subscribers[type];
        else
        {
```

```
            subscribersList = new List<Delegate>();
            _subscribers[type] = subscribersList;
        }
        subscribersList.Add(receivedCallback);
    }
}
```

This implementation is very naive. It just holds a dictionary of `Type`, and callbacks to call for that type. If systems adding a subscriber to this needs to go out of scope and get collected, this prevents it. There are typically two things I'd do to this: add a `Unsubscribe` method and let the `SubscribeTo` method return something that identifies the subscription for the `Unsubscribe`. Secondly, the callbacks should be wrapped with `WeakReference`, which is something .NET supports. The callback mechanism allows you to check whether the reference is alive, and if not, clean it up. We're basically proving the concepts at this stage, and this book does not have the goal of implementing all the moving parts in a typical MVVM solution on Xamarin. There are a few libraries out there that deal with this, such as MvvmCross, MVVM Light, and soon also Bifrost. I would recommend taking a look at these.

DelegateCommand

The second building block we are going to need, or at least want to have for convenience, is something called `DelegateCommand`. The purpose of this is to be able to simply create an `ICommand` instance from a method in our ViewModels. Add a class called `DelegateCommand` in the common **SignalRChat.Mobile** project.

Make the file look as follows:

```
using System;
using System.Windows.Input;

namespace SignalRChat.Mobile
{
    public delegate bool CanExecuteEventHandler<T>(T parameter);

    public delegate void ExecuteEventHandler<T>(T parameter);

    public delegate bool CanExecuteWithoutParameterEventHandler();
```

```
       public delegate void ExecuteWithoutParameterEventHandler();

       public class DelegateCommand<T> : DelegateCommand
       {
           public ExecuteEventHandler<T> ExecuteEventHandler { get;
private set; }
           public CanExecuteEventHandler<T> CanExecuteEventHandler { get;
private set; }

           public DelegateCommand(ExecuteEventHandler<T>
executeEventHandler)
               : this(executeEventHandler, null)
           {

           }

           public DelegateCommand(ExecuteEventHandler<T>
executeEventHandler, CanExecuteEventHandler<T> canExecuteEventHandler)
           {
               ExecuteEventHandler = executeEventHandler;
               CanExecuteEventHandler = canExecuteEventHandler;
           }


           public override bool CanExecute(object parameter)
           {
               if (null == CanExecuteEventHandler)
               {
                   return true;
               }
               return CanExecuteEventHandler((T)parameter);
           }

           public override void Execute(object parameter)
           {
               if (null != ExecuteEventHandler)
               {
                   ExecuteEventHandler((T)parameter);
               }
           }

           public override Type ExecuteTargetType
           {
```

```
        get
        {
            return ExecuteEventHandler.Target.GetType();
        }
    }

    public override Type CanExecuteTargetType
    {
        get
        {
            return CanExecuteEventHandler.Target.GetType();
        }
    }

}

public class DelegateCommand : ICommand
{
    public ExecuteWithoutParameterEventHandler
ExecuteWithoutParameterEventHandler { get; private set; }
    public CanExecuteWithoutParameterEventHandler
CanExecuteWithoutParameterEventHandler { get; private set; }

    protected DelegateCommand()
    {
    }

    public DelegateCommand(ExecuteWithoutParameterEventHandler
executeWithoutParameterEventHandler)
        : this(executeWithoutParameterEventHandler, null)
    {

    }

    public DelegateCommand(ExecuteWithoutParameterEventHandler
executeWithoutParameterEventHandler,
                            CanExecuteWithoutParameterEventHandler
canExecuteWithoutParameterEventHandler)
    {
        ExecuteWithoutParameterEventHandler =
executeWithoutParameterEventHandler;
```

```
                        CanExecuteWithoutParameterEventHandler =
        canExecuteWithoutParameterEventHandler;
            }

        public event EventHandler CanExecuteChanged;
        public virtual bool CanExecute(object parameter)
        {
            if (null == CanExecuteWithoutParameterEventHandler)
            {
                return true;
            }
            return CanExecuteWithoutParameterEventHandler();
        }

        public virtual void Execute(object parameter)
        {
            if (null != ExecuteWithoutParameterEventHandler)
            {
                ExecuteWithoutParameterEventHandler();
            }
        }


        protected void OnCanExecuteChanged()
        {
            if (null != CanExecuteChanged)
            {
                CanExecuteChanged(this, new EventArgs());
            }
        }


        public static DelegateCommand Create(ExecuteEventHandler<obje
ct> execute)
        {
            return new DelegateCommand<object>(execute);
        }

        public static DelegateCommand Create(ExecuteEventHandler<obje
ct> execute, CanExecuteEventHandler<object> canExecute)
        {
```

```
            return new DelegateCommand<object>(execute, canExecute);
        }

        public static DelegateCommand Create(ExecuteWithoutParameterEv
entHandler execute)
        {
            return new DelegateCommand(execute);

        }

        public static DelegateCommand Create(ExecuteWithoutParameterEv
entHandler execute, CanExecuteWithoutParameterEventHandler canExecute)
        {
            return new DelegateCommand(execute, canExecute);
        }

        public static DelegateCommand Create<T>(ExecuteEventHandler<T>
execute)
        {
            return new DelegateCommand<T>(execute);
        }

        public static DelegateCommand Create<T>(ExecuteEventHandler<T>
execute, CanExecuteEventHandler<T> canExecute)
        {
            return new DelegateCommand<T>(execute, canExecute);
        }


        public virtual Type ExecuteTargetType
        {
            get
            {
                return ExecuteWithoutParameterEventHandler.Target.
GetType();
            }
        }

        public virtual Type CanExecuteTargetType
        {
            get
            {
```

```
                    return CanExecuteWithoutParameterEventHandler.Target.
GetType();
                }
            }
        }
    }
}
```

Now, with the building blocks in place, we can move on to the code for the solution. Let's start with the SignalR code. This code will basically be the same as in the WPF sample. The client code is very consistent. You could in fact argue that we should have created what is called a **PCL** (**Portable Class Library**) and shared most of the code between all .NET-based clients. This is something we actually could have done; in fact, we could have even shared the ViewModels across desktop and mobile as well. However, for the sake of simplicity, we will just recreate things directly for the mobile project.

Security

We need to log into the solution and get the right cookies back; the interface for this is the same as in the WPF client, but the implementation differs slightly:

1. Create an interface called `ISecurity` in the common **SignalRChat.Mobile** project.

2. Make the file look as follows:

```
using System.Net;

namespace SignalRChat.Mobile
{
    public interface ISecurity
    {
        CookieContainer CookieContainer { get; }

        bool Authenticate(string userName, string password);
    }
}
```

3. Add an implementation of this interface called `Security`. Make the file look as follows:

```
using System;
using System.Collections.Generic;
using System.Net;
```

```csharp
using System.Net.Http;

namespace SignalRChat.Mobile
{
    public class Security : ISecurity
    {
        const string Site = "http://10.211.55.4:3705";

        public CookieContainer CookieContainer { get; private set;
}

        public bool Authenticate(string userName, string password)
        {
            var postData = new List<KeyValuePair<string,
string>>();
            postData.Add(new KeyValuePair<string,
string>("userName", userName));
            postData.Add(new KeyValuePair<string,
string>("password", password));

            var content = new FormUrlEncodedContent(postData);

            CookieContainer = new CookieContainer();

            var handler = new HttpClientHandler { CookieContainer
= CookieContainer };

            var client = new HttpClient(handler);
            try
            {
                var result = client.PostAsync(Site+"/
SecurityHandler.ashx", content).Result;
                result.EnsureSuccessStatusCode();
            } catch( Exception )
            {
                return false;
            }

            return true;
        }
    }
}
```

Make sure the Site const reflects the URL of your Windows
machine with the IP address we found earlier.

ChatHub

As with the WPF client, we want to have a strongly typed representation of our
Hub in the client. Since we don't have proxy generation for this, we will manually
create it:

1. Create an interface representing the hub called IChatHub in the common
    SignalRChat.Mobile project.

2. Make the file look as follows:

```
using System;
using Microsoft.AspNet.SignalR.Client;

namespace SignalRChat.Mobile
{
    public interface IChatHub
    {
        event Action<StateChange> StateChanged;
        event Action<string> JoinedRoom;
        event Action<string> RoomAdded;
        event Action<string> MessageReceived;

        string CurrentChatRoom { get; }
        void Join(string room);
        void CreateRoom(string room);
        void Send(string message);
    }
}
```

3. Add a class called ChatHub alongside the IChatHub file, and make it look as
    follows:

```
using System;
using Microsoft.AspNet.SignalR.Client;
using Microsoft.AspNet.SignalR.Client.Transports;

namespace SignalRChat.Mobile
{
```

```
public class ChatHub : IChatHub
{
    const string Site = "http://10.211.55.4:3705";

    public event Action<StateChange> StateChanged = (state) =>
{ };
    public event Action<string> JoinedRoom = (room) => { };
    public event Action<string> RoomAdded = (room) => { };
    public event Action<string> MessageReceived = (message) =>
{ };

    HubConnection _hubConnection;
    ISecurity _security;
    IHubProxy _chatProxy;

    public ChatHub(IMessenger messenger, ISecurity security)
    {
        _security = security;
        messenger.SubscribeTo<LoggedIn>(LoggedIn);
    }

    void LoggedIn(LoggedIn loggedIn)
    {
        _hubConnection = new HubConnection(Site);

        _hubConnection.CookieContainer = _security.
CookieContainer;
        _hubConnection.StateChanged += (s) => StateChanged(s);

        _chatProxy = _hubConnection.CreateHubProxy("chat");
        _chatProxy.On("addMessage", (string message) =>
MessageReceived(message));
        _chatProxy.On("addChatRoom", (string room) =>
RoomAdded(room));

        CurrentChatRoom = "Lobby";
        JoinedRoom(CurrentChatRoom);

        _hubConnection.Start().Wait();
    }

    public void Join(string room)
    {
```

```
        _chatProxy.Invoke("Join", room).Wait();
        JoinedRoom(room);
    }

    public void CreateRoom(string room)
    {
        _chatProxy.Invoke("CreateChatRoom", room).Wait();
        JoinedRoom(room);
    }

    public void Send(string message)
    {
        _chatProxy.Invoke("Send", message);
    }

    public string CurrentChatRoom
    {
        get { return (string)_chatProxy["currentChatRoom"]; }
        private set { _chatProxy["currentChatRoom"] = value; }
    }
}
}
```

 Make sure the Site const reflects the URL of your Windows machine with the IP address we found earlier.

Login

The first screen that we are going to have the user go through will be the login screen:

1. Right-click on the common **SignalRChat.Mobile** project and select **Add | New Item**. In the **Add New Item** dialog box, select the **Forms Xaml Page** and name it Login.xaml.

2. Make the XML in the newly created file look as follows:

```
<?xml version="1.0" encoding="utf-8" ?>
<ContentPage xmlns="http://xamarin.com/schemas/2014/forms"
             xmlns:x="http://schemas.microsoft.com/winfx/2009/
xaml"
```

```
                              x:Class="SignalRChat.Mobile.Login">


  <StackLayout Orientation="Vertical" VerticalOptions="Start"
Padding="8,32,8,8">

    <Label Text="UserName"/>
    <Entry Keyboard="Text" Placeholder="Enter username"
Text="{Binding UserName, Mode=TwoWay}" />
    <Label Text="Password"/>
    <Entry Keyboard="Text" IsPassword="true" Placeholder="Enter
password" Text="{Binding Password, Mode=TwoWay}"/>

    <Button Command="{Binding LoginCommand}" Text="Login"></
Button>

  </StackLayout>
</ContentPage>
```

The bindings are relative to what is called `BindingContext`. Unlike WPF and most XAML platforms, it is not called **DataContext**. We're going to see how we wire this up soon.

3. We are now going to need the ViewModel that the view will consume. Add a file called `LoginViewModel.cs` and make it look as follows:

```
using System.Windows.Input;
using Xamarin.Forms;

namespace SignalRChat.Mobile
{
    public class LoginViewModel
    {
        INavigation _navigation;
        ISecurity _security;
        IMessenger _messenger;

        public LoginViewModel(INavigation navigation, ISecurity
security, IMessenger messenger)
        {
            _navigation = navigation;
            _security = security;
            _messenger = messenger;
```

```
                LoginCommand = DelegateCommand.Create(Login);
        }

        public string UserName { get; set; }
        public string Password { get; set; }
        public ICommand LoginCommand { get; private set; }

        public void Login()
        {
            if (_security.Authenticate(UserName, Password))
            {
                var navigationPage = new NavigationPage();
                App.Navigation = navigationPage.Navigation;
                navigationPage.PushAsync(new ChatRooms());

                _navigation.PushModalAsync(navigationPage);

                _messenger.Publish(new LoggedIn());
            }
        }
    }
}
```

We're taking in a dependency to INavigation. This is an interface from Xamarin.Forms that we're using to navigate in the application. In addition to this, we're also taking in the messenger that we created earlier and as you can see, we are publishing the LoggedIn message that we will create in a bit. It is also using something called ChatRooms that is also coming later.

4. Add a class called LoggedIn to the same common project. We don't need anything in this class, so just leave it empty, save it, and close the file.

5. Go to the App.cs in the **SignalRChat.Mobile** project and make it look as follows:

```
using System;
using System.Collections.Generic;
using System.Linq;
using System.Text;
using SimpleInjector;
using Xamarin.Forms;

namespace SignalRChat.Mobile
{
```

```
public class App : Application
{
    public static readonly Container Container;
    public static INavigation Navigation;

    static App()
    {
        Container = new Container();

        var security = new Security();
        var messenger = new Messenger();
        var chatHub = new ChatHub(messenger, security);
        Container.Register<ISecurity>(()=>security, Lifestyle.
Singleton);
        Container.Register<IChatHub>(() => chatHub, Lifestyle.
Singleton);
        Container.Register<IMessenger>(() => messenger,
Lifestyle.Singleton);
        Container.Register<INavigation>(() => Navigation);
    }


    public App()
    {
        // The root page of your application
        MainPage = new Login();
    }

    protected override void OnStart()
    {
        // Handle when your app starts
    }

    protected override void OnSleep()
    {
        // Handle when your app sleeps
    }

    protected override void OnResume()
    {
        // Handle when your app resumes
    }
}
}
```

We set the `MainPage` to the Login page. This will then navigate directly to it. In addition, the static constructor sets up the `SimpleInjector` IoC container and configures it correctly for the dependencies we are going to use. The navigation field is being set outside of this file—this is not something I would normally recommend doing, but in the interest of not overcomplicating things, we will do this. In general, I would recommend figuring out a better way to resolve this lazily from a delegate callback or similar.

6. Right-click on the `Login.xaml` file and select **View Code**. Make it look as follows:

```
using Xamarin.Forms;

namespace SignalRChat.Mobile
{
    public partial class Login : ContentPage
    {
        public Login()
        {
            InitializeComponent();

            var security = App.Container.GetInstance<ISecurity>();
            var messenger = App.Container.
GetInstance<IMessenger>();
            var viewModel = new LoginViewModel(Navigation,
security, messenger);
            BindingContext = viewModel;
        }
    }
}
```

Basically, we ask the IoC container using it as a ServiceLocator. This is often seen as an anti-pattern, and I generally agree with it. We want dependencies to be injected. However, in a book like this, we have to take a couple of shortcuts to keep focus on the important things. The usage of an IoC is not needed, but it is put in to show how I go about thinking of development. Make note of `BindingContext`; we take the ViewModel instance and set it directly. By doing this, all the bindings will be activated.

ChatRooms

We are not going to be able to compile nor run just yet. We will need to complete the entire application in order for us to do so:

1. Right-click on the common **SignalRChat.Mobile** project and select **Add | New Item**. In the **Add New Item** dialog box, select the **Forms Xaml Page** and name it ChatRooms.xaml.

2. Make the file look as follows:

```xml
<?xml version="1.0" encoding="utf-8" ?>
<ContentPage xmlns="http://xamarin.com/schemas/2014/forms"
             xmlns:x="http://schemas.microsoft.com/winfx/2009/
xaml"
             xmlns:local="clr-namespace:SignalRChat.
Mobile;assembly=SignalrChat.Mobile"
             x:Class="SignalRChat.Mobile.ChatRooms"
             Title="Rooms">

  <StackLayout Orientation="Vertical" Padding="8">

    <StackLayout Orientation="Horizontal">
      <Entry Keyboard="Text" Placeholder="Enter room" HorizontalOp
tions="FillAndExpand" Text="{Binding Room, Mode=TwoWay}"/>
      <Button Command="{Binding AddRoomCommand}" Text="Send"
HorizontalOptions="End"/>
    </StackLayout>

    <ListView ItemsSource="{Binding Rooms}" SelectedItem="{Binding
CurrentRoom, Mode=TwoWay}">
      <ListView.ItemTemplate>
        <DataTemplate>
          <TextCell Text="{Binding}"/>
        </DataTemplate>
      </ListView.ItemTemplate>
    </ListView>
  </StackLayout>
</ContentPage>
```

3. We are now going to need the ViewModel that the view will consume.
    Add a file called ChatRoomsViewModel.cs and make it look as follows:

```csharp
using System;
using System.Collections.ObjectModel;
using System.Windows.Input;
using Xamarin.Forms;

namespace SignalRChat.Mobile
{
    public class ChatRoomsViewModel
    {
        string _currentRoom;
        INavigation _navigation;
        IChatHub _chatHub;

        public ChatRoomsViewModel(INavigation navigation, IChatHub
chatHub)
        {
            _navigation = navigation;
            _chatHub = chatHub;
            Rooms = new ObservableCollection<string>();

            chatHub.RoomAdded += (room) => Device.
BeginInvokeOnMainThread(() => Rooms.Add(room));

            AddRoomCommand = DelegateCommand.Create(AddRoom);
        }

        public string CurrentRoom
        {
            get { return _currentRoom; }
            set
            {
                _currentRoom = value;
                _chatHub.Join(value);
                _navigation.PushAsync(new Chat(value));
            }
        }

        public ObservableCollection<String> Rooms { get; private
set; }

        public ICommand AddRoomCommand { get; private set; }
```

```
        public string Room { get; set; }

        public void AddRoom()
        {
            _chatHub.CreateRoom(Room);
        }
    }
}
```

4. Right-click on the `ChatRooms.xaml` file and select **View Code**. Make it look as follows:

```
using SimpleInjector;
using Xamarin.Forms;

namespace SignalRChat.Mobile
{
    public partial class ChatRooms : ContentPage
    {
        public ChatRooms()
        {
            InitializeComponent();

            BindingContext = App.Container.GetInstance<ChatRoomsVi
ewModel>();
        }
    }
}
```

Chat

The last component is the actual chat. The `ChatRoom` class navigates to the chat with the selected room:

1. Right-click on the common **SignalRChat.Mobile** project and select **Add | New Item**. In the **Add New Item** dialog box, select the **Forms Xaml Page** and name it `Chat.xaml`.

2. Make the file look as follows:

```
<?xml version="1.0" encoding="utf-8" ?>
<ContentPage xmlns="http://xamarin.com/schemas/2014/forms"
             xmlns:x="http://schemas.microsoft.com/winfx/2009/
xaml"
```

```
                x:Class="SignalRChat.Mobile.Chat"
                Title="{Binding Room}">
  <StackLayout Orientation="Vertical" Padding="8">

    <StackLayout Orientation="Horizontal">
        <Entry x:Name="room" Keyboard="Text" Placeholder="Enter
message" HorizontalOptions="FillAndExpand" Text="{Binding Message,
Mode=TwoWay}"/>
        <Button Command="{Binding SendCommand}" Text="Send"
HorizontalOptions="End"/>
    </StackLayout>

    <ListView ItemsSource="{Binding Messages}">
      <ListView.ItemTemplate>
        <DataTemplate>
          <TextCell Text="{Binding}"/>
        </DataTemplate>
      </ListView.ItemTemplate>
    </ListView>
  </StackLayout>
</ContentPage>
```

3. Open up the code-behind of the Chat.xaml file by right-clicking on it in the **Solution Explorer** and selecting **View Code**.

4. Let's add the following constructors to it:

```
public Chat() : this("Unknown") {}

public Chat(string room)
{
    InitializeComponent();

    var chatHub = App.Container.GetInstance<IChatHub>();
    BindingContext = new ChatViewModel(room, chatHub);
}
```

 Every room we go into will get a new view and ViewModel for the room. We explicitly have to initialize the ViewModel like this, by calling the IoC container to get an instance of the IChatHub.

5. We are now going to need the ViewModel that the view will consume.
   Add a file called `ChatViewModel.cs` and make it look as follows:

```csharp
using System.Collections.ObjectModel;
using System.Windows.Input;
using Xamarin.Forms;

namespace SignalRChat.Mobile
{
    public class ChatViewModel
    {
        IChatHub _chatHub;

        public ChatViewModel(string room, IChatHub chatHub)
        {
            Room = room;
            _chatHub = chatHub;
            Messages = new ObservableCollection<string>();

            SendCommand = DelegateCommand.Create(Send);

            chatHub.MessageReceived += (message) => Device.
BeginInvokeOnMainThread(() => Messages.Add(message));
        }

        public string Room { get; private set; }
        public string Message { get; set; }
        public ICommand SendCommand { get; private set; }

        public ObservableCollection<string> Messages { get;
private set; }

        public void Send()
        {
            _chatHub.Send(Message);
        }
    }
}
```

The result

The solution should now be possible to compile and run. First, you need to set the Web project as the startup project and then run it so that the server is ready. Once you have it running, you can set the iOS project again as the startup project and then run it.

You should then be presented with the login screen:

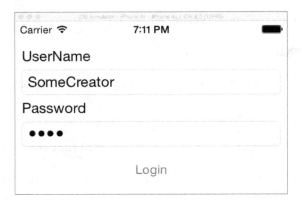

After logging in with the credentials that the server is configured with, you will get to the **Rooms** page. You can select a room from the list or create a new one:

Once in the room, you can send messages and also receive messages:

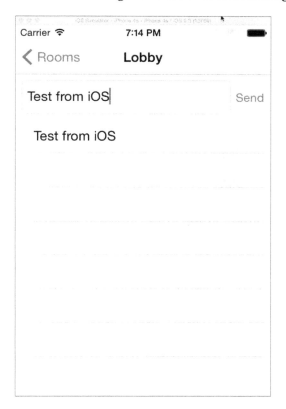

Having the web browser and the iOS emulator side by side should give you the same data going back and forth between them, when either of the clients are in use:

The **Room** list should look as follows:

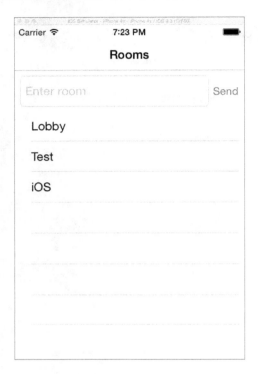

Summary

Xamarin has matured over the years, and with their recent embracing of XAML, they are building on the great things that XAML has going for it. It is truly becoming a write once, run many type of platform. With Visual Studio 2015, Xamarin even comes as part of the out-of-the-box experience, proving the maturity of the platform and also the Microsoft's commitment to work with Xamarin in order to give us, as developers, the best tools for the job.

In the next chapter, we will see how you can debug things and figure out when there are problems in a good way.

10
Monitoring

This chapter will show tools that exist to help you know what is going on in your SignalR-enabled system. Until now, SignalR has been a black box, which is fine until things start failing. Then comes monitoring that helps us pinpoint any problems. Monitoring allows you to look under the hood and get the facts about what is going on, thus helping you to diagnose your solution. Sometimes, it is not that obvious as to what causes a problem, especially when moving into a single page application development; this shift of looking at postbacks looks at the traffic between the server and the client. With the right tools and know-hows, this shouldn't be a problem.

In this chapter, we will cover the following topics:

- Enabling tracing or logging
- Using Fiddler and Charles
- Enabling performance counters
- Getting debug info into Visual Studio
- Chrome Developer Tools

Logging

Perhaps one of the most efficient debugging tools is logging; just get the text out that says what is going on in your system. Logging is the age-old technique of putting in code that writes out text to know what the system is doing. SignalR has a great support for this in all tiers.

Logging on the server side

You simply enable logging on the server by adding configuration to the application configuration file (`App.config` or `Web.config`) depending on the project type. In the configuration, you specify what events you are interested in seeing. You can also specify where you want it to log to, such as a text file, the Windows event log, or a custom log, using an implementation of `TraceListener`. The following table shows what trace sources are available and a description of what they represent:

Source	Messages
`SignalR.SqlMessageBus`	This scales out the setup, database operation, error, and timeout events
`SignalR.ServiceBusMessageBus`	This scales out provider topic creation and subscription, error, and messaging events
`SignalR.RedisMessageBus`	This scales out provider connection, disconnection, and error events
`SignalR.ScaleoutMessageBus`	This scales out messaging events
`SignalR.Transports.WebSocketTransport`	This transports connection, disconnection, messaging, and error events
`SignalR.Transports.ServerSentEventsTransport`	This transports connection, disconnection, messaging, and error events
`SignalR.Transports.ForeverFrameTransport`	This transports connection, disconnection, messaging, and error events
`SignalR.Transports.LongPollingTransport`	This transports connection, disconnection, messaging, and error events
`SignalR.Transports.TransportHeartBeat`	This transport connection, disconnection, messaging, and error events
`SignalR.ReflectedHubDescriptorProvider`	This reflects the hub discovery events

To enable this, you can add the following code to your application config file (`App.config` or `Web.config`) within the `configuration` tag of one of these files:

```
<system.diagnostics>
  <sources>
    <source name="SignalR.SqlMessageBus">
      <listeners>
        <add name="SignalR-Bus" />
      </listeners>
    </source>
    <source name="SignalR.ServiceBusMessageBus">
      <listeners>
        <add name="SignalR-Bus" />
      </listeners>
    </source>
    <source name="SignalR.RedisMessageBus">
      <listeners>
        <add name="SignalR-Bus" />
      </listeners>
    </source>
    <source name="SignalR.ScaleoutMessageBus">
      <listeners>
        <add name="SignalR-Bus" />
      </listeners>
    </source>
    <source name="SignalR.Transports.WebSocketTransport">
      <listeners>
        <add name="SignalR-Transports" />
      </listeners>
    </source>
    <source name="SignalR.Transports.ServerSentEventsTransport">
      <listeners>
        <add name="SignalR-Transports" />
      </listeners>
    </source>
    <source name="SignalR.Transports.ForeverFrameTransport">
      <listeners>
        <add name="SignalR-Transports" />
      </listeners>
    </source>
    <source name="SignalR.Transports.LongPollingTransport">
```

```xml
        <listeners>
          <add name="SignalR-Transports" />
        </listeners>
      </source>
      <source name="SignalR.Transports.TransportHeartBeat">
        <listeners>
          <add name="SignalR-Transports" />
        </listeners>
      </source>
      <source name="SignalR.ReflectedHubDescriptorProvider">
        <listeners>
          <add name="SignalR-Init" />
        </listeners>
      </source>
    </sources>
    <!-- Sets the trace verbosity level -->
    <switches>
      <add name="SignalRSwitch" value="Verbose" />
    </switches>
    <!-- Specifies the trace writer for output -->
    <sharedListeners>
      <!-- Listener for transport events -->
      <add name="SignalR-Transports" type="System.Diagnostics.
TextWriterTraceListener" initializeData="transports.log.txt" />
      <!-- Listener for scaleout provider events -->
      <add name="SignalR-Bus" type="System.Diagnostics.
TextWriterTraceListener" initializeData="bus.log.txt" />
      <!-- Listener for hub discovery events -->
      <add name="SignalR-Init" type="System.Diagnostics.
TextWriterTraceListener" initializeData="init.log.txt" />
    </sharedListeners>
    <trace autoflush="true" />
  </system.diagnostics>
```

Running an application with this should yield something similar in the `transports.log.txt` file. Typically, this file is located in your application bin output folder, whereas for a web application, it's in the root of the web application:

In Windows, we have the Windows event log, in which the system itself registers events that occur, but it's also a place where applications can post to. This is often used by IT to monitor what goes on. Popular toolsets out there can use this to alert IT when something happens. To get the same logging into the Windows event log, you simply need to change the listeners as follows:

```
<sharedListeners>
  <!-- Listener for transport events -->
  <add name="SignalR-Transports" type="System.Diagnostics.
EventLogTraceListener" initializeData="SignalRScaleoutLog" />
  <!-- Listener for scaleout provider events -->
  <add name="SignalR-Bus" type="System.Diagnostics.
EventLogTraceListener" initializeData="SignalRTransportLog" />
  <!-- Listener for hub discovery events -->
  <add name="SignalR-Init" type="System.Diagnostics.
EventLogTraceListener" initializeData="SignalRInitLog" />
</sharedListeners>
```

The easiest way to see the result is to open the event viewer in Windows. This is accessible by pressing Windows key + *R*, and entering `eventvwr` in it, as shown here:

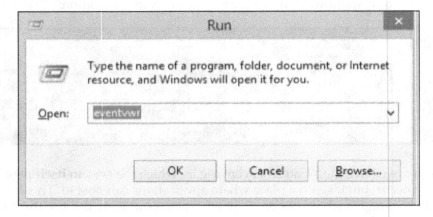

Once it is opened, you should then see events, as shown in the following screenshot:

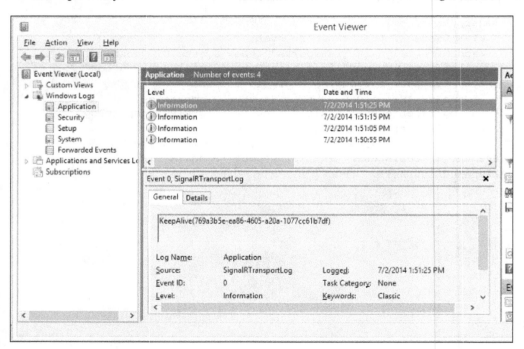

To keep the level of events in the event log to a manageable level, you should set `TraceLevel` to `Error`.

Logging in the JavaScript client

The server side will only tell you parts of the truth; you might run into issues in the client as well. Enabling this is very simple.

If you are using the generated proxies for the Hubs, you can simply enable it with the following code:

```
$.connection.hub.logging = true;
$.connection.hub.start();
```

If you're not using the proxies, you can enable it as follows:

```
var connection = $.hubConnection();
connection.logging = true;
connection.start();
```

In the browser's developer tools in the **Console** output, you should be seeing something similar to the following screenshot. The developer tools are typically available by pressing the *F12* button on your keyboard. For some browsers, you might need to enable it in the settings of the browser:

```
Console  Search  Emulation  Rendering
⊘  ▽  <top frame>  ▼  ☐ Preserve log
   [15:27:19 GMT+0100 (Romance Standard Time)] SignalR: Client subscribed to hub    jquery.signalR-2.1.0.min.js:8
   'threadhub'.
   [15:27:19 GMT+0100 (Romance Standard Time)] SignalR: Negotiating with    jquery.signalR-2.1.0.min.js:8
   '/signalr/negotiate?clientProtocol=1.4&connectionData=%5B%7B%22name%22%3A%22threadhub%22%7D%5D'.
   [15:27:19 GMT+0100 (Romance Standard Time)] SignalR: Connecting to websocket endpoint    jquery.signalR-2.1.0.min.js:8
   'ws://localhost:34403/signalr/connect?
   transport=webSockets&clientProtocol=1.4&connectionToken=kxo8n1nuMAPpS26uE%2BxyVg%2BmuQ2DjnuAbABw40%2F%2B7584IjPBxdoXBgF2
   fd2XRFYn1D579rDMpqKRmi%2Bq4FFLB%2Bn7S06CSV3%2Bym5QG2cLoIXt75irGdvzG05J9LoLY8zsAg1TZzS2Wp69fD529bkiCg%3D%3D&connectionDat
   a=%5B%7B%22name%22%3A%22threadhub%22%7D%5D&tid=4'.
   [15:27:19 GMT+0100 (Romance Standard Time)] SignalR: Websocket opened.    jquery.signalR-2.1.0.min.js:8
   [15:27:19 GMT+0100 (Romance Standard Time)] SignalR: Now monitoring keep alive with a    jquery.signalR-2.1.0.min.js:8
   warning timeout of 13333.333333333332 and a connection lost timeout of 20000.
   [15:27:19 GMT+0100 (Romance Standard Time)] SignalR: Invoking threadhub.GetAll    jquery.signalR-2.1.0.min.js:8
   [15:27:19 GMT+0100 (Romance Standard Time)] SignalR: Invoked threadhub.GetAll    jquery.signalR-2.1.0.min.js:8
>  |
```

Logging in the .NET client

In a regular .NET client, this is just as simple, as shown in the following code:

```
var hubConnection = new HubConnection("http://localhost:9044/");
hubConnection.TraceLevel = TraceLevels.All;
hubConnection.TraceWriter = Console.Out;
await hubConnection.Start();
```

> With C# 5.0, we get the async/await paradigm. This has the new keywords to help us with asynchronous tasks. Earlier, we had used .Wait() on the returning task of an asynchronous method. With the async and await keywords, we can get a clearer way of doing this. The only drawback of this is that the keywords bleed through your API. Be aware of this and you should be fine.

The `TraceWriter` is set to output to the console; this can be customized to be outputting to a file instead, if you want, as shown here:

```
var hubConnection = new HubConnection("http://localhost:9044/");
var writer = new StreamWriter("client.log.txt");
writer.AutoFlush = true;
hubConnection.TraceLevel = TraceLevels.All;
hubConnection.TraceWriter = writer;
await hubConnection.Start();
```

The file would then be written to the place it runs from. By default, this is the binary output folder of the project. Once you run with this, you should see the following output:

```
client.log.txt
1  19:41:39.9103763 - null - ChangeState(Disconnected, Connecting)
2  19:41:40.3750726 - dd61fd48-d796-4518-b36b-ec1dcb970d72 - WS Connecting to: ws:/
3  19:41:40.4442923 - dd61fd48-d796-4518-b36b-ec1dcb970d72 - WS: OnMessage({"C":"d-
4  19:41:40.4874324 - dd61fd48-d796-4518-b36b-ec1dcb970d72 - ChangeState(Connecting
5  19:41:47.4511770 - dd61fd48-d796-4518-b36b-ec1dcb970d72 - WS: OnMessage({"C":"d-
6  19:41:47.4576968 - dd61fd48-d796-4518-b36b-ec1dcb970d72 - WS: OnMessage({"I":"0"
7  19:41:50.3959119 - dd61fd48-d796-4518-b36b-ec1dcb970d72 - WS: OnMessage({})
8  19:41:50.8928084 - dd61fd48-d796-4518-b36b-ec1dcb970d72 - WS: OnMessage({"C":"d-
9
```

Logging from the Xamarin client

The API for the Xamarin is pretty much exactly the same as for the .NET client, so enabling it also very similar. There is, however, not a regular console, so we need a different writer. The simplest thing is then to get it into the output window in Visual Studio. All we need then is to implement `TextWriter` that can actually do this, as shown in the following code:

```
public class DebugTextWriter : TextWriter
{
    StringBuilder _messageBuilder;

    public DebugTextWriter()
    {
        _messageBuilder = new StringBuilder();
    }

    public override void Write(char value)
    {
        switch (value)
        {
            case '\n':
                return;
            case '\r':
                Debug.WriteLine(_messageBuilder.ToString());
                _messageBuilder.Clear();
                return;
            default:
                _messageBuilder.Append(value);
                break;
        }
    }

    public override void Write(string value)
    {
        Debug.WriteLine(value);

    }
    #region implemented abstract members of TextWriter
```

```
public override Encoding Encoding
{
    get { throw new NotImplementedException(); }
}
#endregion
}
```

Then, you need the following when initializing the Hub:

```
var hubConnection = new HubConnection("http://localhost:9044/");
hubConnection.TraceLevel = TraceLevels.All;
hubConnection.TraceWriter = new DebugTextWriter();
await hubConnection.Start();
```

This should yield an output similar to the following:

The same writer could be used in a regular .NET application as well, which is a great way for a developer to see things while working.

Digging deeper into the communication

Logging is really helpful and can really save you a lot of time to figure out what is going on. However, sometimes, you need to go even deeper. At times, you need to look at the raw traffic. There are a few ways of doing this.

Looking under the cover with Fiddler

A popular, free, and very good debugging tool to debug HTTP traffic is Fiddler. You can download it for free at http://www.telerik.com/fiddler. It gives you the opportunity to monitor all HTTP requests happening on your computer.

Fiddler sets itself as a proxy between all traffic and in order to get the best experience from it, you need to enable streams, otherwise SignalR will fall back to long-polling, but not immediately (typically after 3-5 seconds), as shown in the following screenshot:

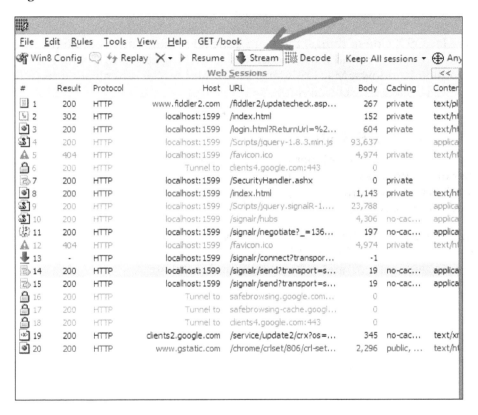

If the browser and server support web sockets, SignalR might choose to use this as its preferred transport. In this case, you want to open up the **Log** tab, as shown here:

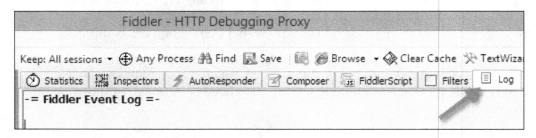

On the Mac OS X side of things, there are quite a few alternatives to do the same thing. The tool that I found most useful was something called as **Charles**. It is supported on Windows, Mac OS X, and Linux, and can be downloaded from here: `http://www.charlesproxy.com/`.

Performance counters

Monitoring messages on a higher level to see the throughput of your application, number of failing messages, and such is vital when putting a system into production. SignalR has a utilities project that gives you performance counters that can be installed on the server(s) that host your application.

The utility is available through NuGet as a package. So right-click on the references of any of the projects and select **Manage NuGet packages**, find the package called `Microsoft ASP.NET SignalR Utilities` and install it:

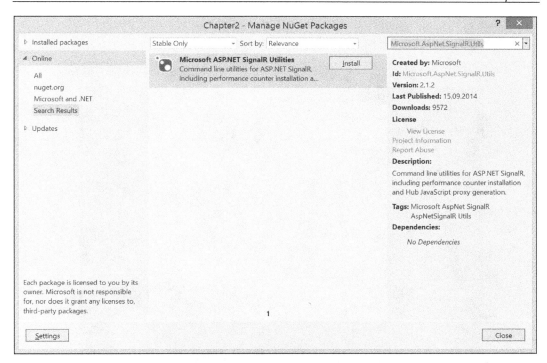

In order to install the performance counters, we need to open a command prompt in Administrator mode.

Navigate to the path of your solution; inside it you should find a folder called `packages`, and inside it a folder called `Microsoft.AspNet.SignalR.Utils.2.1.2` or similar, depending on the version you installed; within this you'll find a folder called **tools**.

Now that you've navigated into all these, enter `signalr ipc` and press *Enter*. This will install all the performance counters:

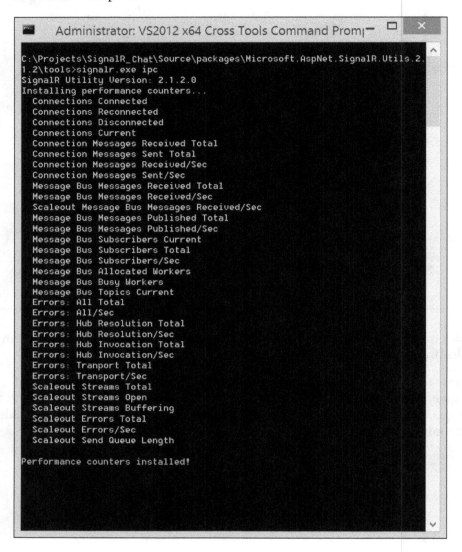

1. To see the performance counters, we need to open perfmon (**Start | Run** or Windows 8, press Windows key + *R*) and type `perfmon` and press *Enter*:

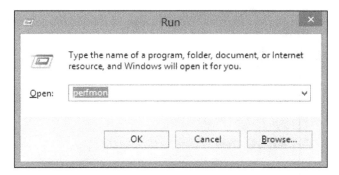

2. Inside `perfmon` you expand the monitoring tools and click on the **Performance Monitor** node and you should see a graph.

3. Click on the big **+** button at the top so that you can add the SignalR counters you want to look at. If you have your application running, you should see it in the **Instances of selected object** filter list:

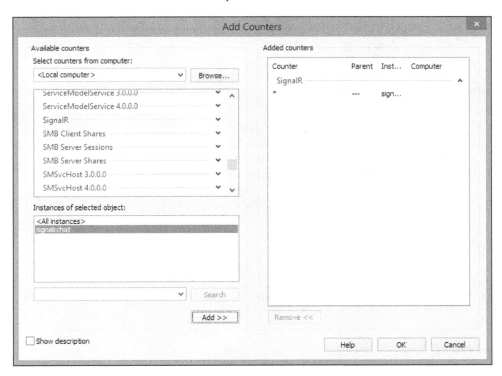

Once added, you can try out the app by sending messages and see the result in the graph:

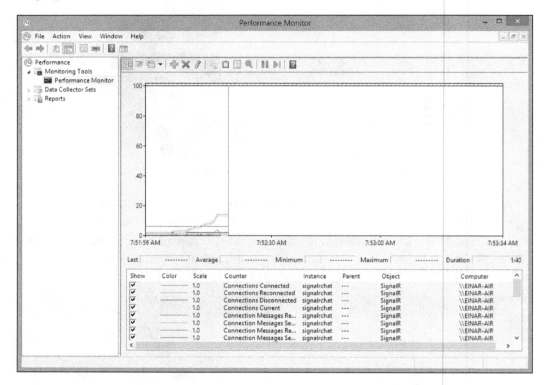

It is really important to disable any performance encounters that you might have enabled for debugging purposes on your production system, as these will cause overhead for all messages. To disable it, you simply enter `signalr upc` in the console from the same folder of the tools in which you enabled it.

Under the cover, inside the browser

Inside all modern web browsers, you should be able to see the network traffic between the client and the server. The browser should be able to show you the details for each transport type. The following screenshot shows how this looks in Chrome for WebSockets transport:

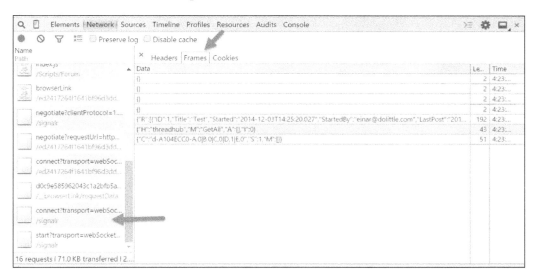

This shows the frames going back and forth for each message being sent either from the client or the server.

Summary

Debugging is not always a matter of attaching the debugger to the server code or the client code and stepping through. Sometimes, the secret is hidden in the data going back and forth and it's not that obvious to understand this with the debugger. With logging enabled, Fiddler, the browser, and the performance counters, you should now be able to both debug and find potential bottlenecks in your system. Although, it might feel a bit primitive compared to the tools that you might be used to when developing vanilla web apps, they are very detailed and should be of great assistance.

In the next chapter, we will look at how to self-host SignalR in your own application.

11
Hosting a Server Using Self-hosted OWIN

This chapter will cover how to host SignalR outside the comfort of a web server. There are occasions where you need to be more lightweight, or simply host things inside a .NET client or similar.

In this chapter, we'll cover the following topics:

- Getting started with self-hosted OWIN
- Connecting a .NET client to the self-hosted server

At this stage, the developer should be familiar with how the server works and how to set it up in their own app. They should have a working sample of the chat working with the OWIN server. The developer should also be familiar with how and why to scale out the messaging aspect of SignalR.

Self-hosting

Sometimes you really don't want to have a big footprint on your application when you're deploying. You don't want to have the IIS dependency or other web server software, you just your own executable and that's it. In combination with OWIN **Open Web Interface for .NET**, SignalR supports this out of the box. OWIN is something to keep an eye on and get your hands dirty with, as this is what will make up the Microsoft web stack moving forward, not only for self-hosting but also for all kinds of hosts. It represents an abstraction that is not linked to any particular environment and makes it easier to move between different environments.

Let's get started by creating a new solution. This time, the focus will be on how to achieve the technical solution of self-hosting and not what the solution does:

1. Open Visual Studio and create a new project (**File | New Project**).

2. Select **Visual C#** from the left-hand side tree and then select **Console Application**. Name the project `Chapter11`:

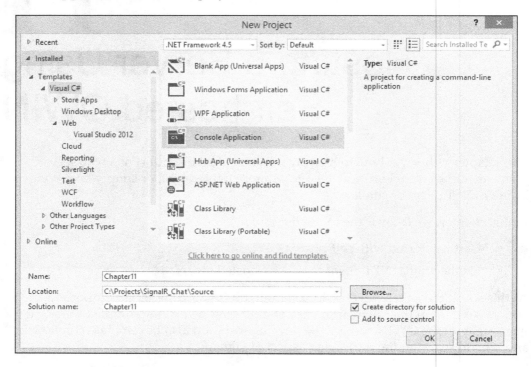

Adding the needed packages

As in the previous chapters, we are now going to pull down a few dependencies from NuGet:

1. Add a NuGet package reference, as described in *Chapter 1*, *The Primer*.

2. Right-click on **References** in **Solution Explorer** and select **Manage NuGet packages**, and type `Microsoft.AspNet.SignalR.SelfHost` into the Search panel.

3. Select it and then click on **Install**.

In addition to this, if you want to enable the self-hosted server to be available for clients coming from other domains, you need to pull down a package called `Microsoft.Owin.Cors`; so add this package as well.

Adding the code needed for self-hosting

As mentioned earlier, this chapter is not focusing on anything from a user's perspective. So we're just going to create the simplest chat that is there (no authentication nor chat rooms or anything)—a chat that only sends messages.

Let's start off with the server and how we initialize it. We will be needing a startup class, as we've seen in the previous solutions, but this time around it won't be created by any package that we have pulled down. In the root of the project, add a C# class file called `Startup.cs`.

Add the following by using the statements at the top:

```
using Microsoft.AspNet.SignalR;
using Microsoft.Owin.Cors;
using Owin;
```

Then, make the class implementation look as follows:

```
public class Startup
{
    public void Configuration(IAppBuilder app)
    {
        app.Map("/signalr", map =>
        {
            app.UseCors(CorsOptions.AllowAll);

            var hubConfiguration = new HubConfiguration
            {
                EnableJSONP = true
            };

            map.RunSignalR(hubConfiguration);
        });
    }
}
```

The first thing we need to do is to host SignalR at the /signalr route, which is default, and we could in fact have been using the map.MapSignalR() method if that's all we wanted to achieve. However, we want to enable cross-domain access for our server. Although this is not going to be used here, it's important to decide if you want to enable any clients from any domain to connected to your solution. The first thing we do is enable it through the .UseCors() method. Then, we tell the hub configuration that allows JavaScript clients to connect using a technique called JSONP. This allows web browsers to do cross-domain communication by telling the server to return JavaScript code that gets executed when the call is done. One reason for this approach is that browsers protect against cross-site scripting in order to avoid code from other domains/servers being added. Another approach is that browsers include malicious scripts that could potentially take over your solution or simply just start recording keystrokes or capture changes in input fields on the page and send these back to the attacker. With this technique, we are circumventing the mechanism that is protecting us by asking it to return data in the form executable JavaScript. When enabling **Cross-Origin Resource Sharing (CORS)**, we tell SignalR to add HTTP headers that provide the browser and the server a way to request remote URLs when they have the permission.

Now, we need to start a host that will then start the SignalR pipeline. Open the Program.cs file. Inside the main() method, place the following code:

```
using( WebApp.Start<Startup>("http://localhost:8181"))
{
    Console.WriteLine("Server running at http://localhost:8181/");
    Console.ReadLine();
}
```

This is all that's needed to get a SignalR server hosted; all we now need is a hub that will expose the logic we want exposed.

Add a new class called `ChatHub.cs` to the root of the project. Make sure you have the following using statements at the top:

```
using System;
using Microsoft.AspNet.SignalR;
```

Make the class look as follows:

```
public class ChatHub : Hub
{
    public void SendMessage(string message)
    {
        Console.WriteLine("Connection {0} : {1}",Context.ConnectionId,
message);
        Clients.AllExcept(Context.ConnectionId).
messageReceived(message);
    }
}
```

All we do is expose a `SendMessage()` method that can be called by any client and it then just sends out that message to the console and to other connected clients.

> Notice the `.AllExcept()` method call. This is really handy if you want to send a message to all the connected clients, except for one or more clients. This method takes a parameter list of connection identifiers. In this particular case, we don't want to send the message back to the sender, we just want to get the incoming connection identifier from the `Context` property.

The client

This was all for the server. We're now going to need a client that can connect and send messages and also receive messages from other connected clients. Let's add a second project to the solution:

1. Right-click on the solution in **Solution Explorer** and navigate to **Add | New Project**:

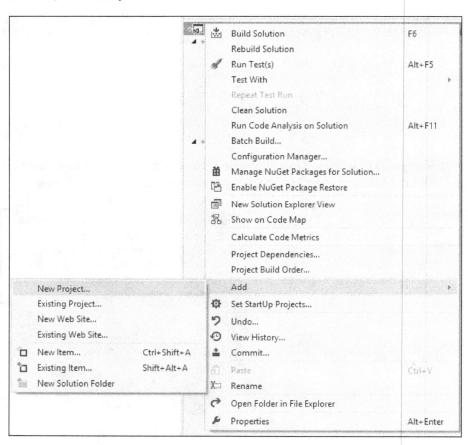

2. Select **Visual C#** from the left-hand side tree and then select **Console Application**. Name the project `Chapter11.Client`:

Again, we will be needing something from good old NuGet. Add a reference to a package called `Microsoft.AspNet.SignalR.Client`. Open up the `Program.cs` file in the client project. Put the following code inside the `Main()` method:

```
var hubConnection = new HubConnection("http://localhost:8181");
var hubProxy = hubConnection.CreateHubProxy("ChatHub");
hubProxy.On("messageReceived", (string message) =>
{
    Console.WriteLine(message);
});

hubConnection.Start().ContinueWith(t=>Console.WriteLine("Connected")).
Wait();
```

```
for (; ; )
{
    var line = Console.ReadLine();
    if (line == "q")
    {
        break;
    }
    hubProxy.Invoke("SendMessage", line);
}
```

As we saw earlier, with both the Windows Phone client libraries and the Xamarin ones, we create `HubConnection` and `HubProxy`. The API is exactly the same, making it very consistent to work with and easy to reuse knowledge.

Running both, and typing `Hello` and hitting the *Enter* key should yield a server to look as follows:

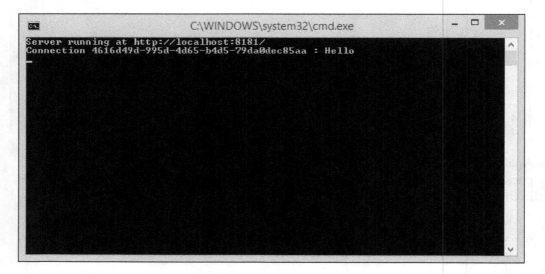

Also, the client should look as follows:

Summary

Hosting any web solution in your own process can be very useful in many scenarios. For instance, let's say you have a legacy Windows app and you are in the process of building a web version of it, but you want to explore new features in the old app before releasing the new one. Hosting these parts on your own using OWIN can then be useful. With the information in this chapter, you should be well on your way to do just that and have SignalR be your transport for communication.

Although SignalR is very technical in its nature, and there are a lot of interesting things it does technically. In my opinion, it is, first and foremost, a tool to increase the user experience. Users today are expecting more from our systems; they've grown accustomed to a certain experience they find in solutions such as Facebook and Twitter, wherein things are delivered almost instantly to them. Through the advances in the mobile space, our users have raised the bar in terms of expectations in general. This is something that even the line of business apps should do their best to accommodate. SignalR is not the only implementation out there.

For platforms other than .NET, there are other options as well. For the .NET space, SignalR is the most well-known and popular one. In fact, I personally have yet to learn about any other solution (not that I have looked under every rock that is there). The point is that I digress what SignalR does, to take away all the nitty-gritty details of how to keep a persistent connection between the client and the server, leaving you as a developer to think about the important things — delivering business value. SignalR gives us the potential to not think about a few technical concepts that we tend to spend time on — concurrency and staleness. Especially, if we break things down into the smallest problem and are able to represent this in a message or a command, we can really start focusing on the business value and our core domain. The concepts behind SignalR are the most important things to take away from SignalR: the messaging, the decoupling of your software, and how you can think differently about the technical problems we tend to impose on our system, such as concurrency and staleness. SignalR really proves that it is possible to take these things out of the equation, enabling us to write better, more responsive, and more user-friendly applications today. By default, my position today is to use SignalR no matter what — I see no point in not using it. In fact, I use it for all the communication going back and forth with the server. Due to its nature, it feels more responsive, and I get new opportunities that I didn't have before.

"RealTime" applications are a different ballgame, and it's about recognizing this rather than the technical aspect of it. I really hope you've enjoyed this book and that it has helped in opening the door to this ballgame.

Index

A

AngularJS 25, 28
authentication 73-80
Authorize 80

B

backplane 90
Bifrost
 about 99, 137
 URL 101

C

Charles
 about 172
 URL 172
chat 117-119
chat application
 defining 22, 39, 40
chat rooms 114-117
client
 defining 3, 40
code signing 131-133
Common Language Runtime (CLR) 127
communication
 defining 170
composition 120-122
connections
 preparing for 134-137
Cross-Origin Resource Sharing (CORS) 182
cross platform 125, 126

D

DataContext 149
decoupling 8, 40, 41
Dependency Inversion Principle
 about 29, 42
 using 97
desktop
 building for 98
Document Object Model (DOM) 14
DotGNU 125

E

emulator
 URL 127
extension methods
 creating 92

F

Fiddler
 defining 171, 172
final puzzle piece
 defining 81, 82
Fody 100

G

groups 49

H

HTTP handler config 71
hub
 securing 80
hub proxy 110-114

I

IIS7 70
Inversion of Control (IoC) 29, 42

J

jQuery 14
JSONP 182

L

life cycle events 46
logging
  about 161
  from Xamarin client 169, 170
  in JavaScript client 167
  in .NET client 168
  on server side 162-167

M

Mac
  using 126-130
Mac, in cloud
  URL 126
Martin Fowlers
  URL 95
Martin Fowlers presentation model
  URL 41
messages, in SignalR
  about 83, 84
  backplane, creating 90, 91
  scaling out, with Azure 87-89
  scaling out, with Redis 86, 87
  scaling out, with SQL Server 84-86
messaging 7
Model View Controller (MVC)
  about 11, 40
  URL 10
Model View ViewModel (MVVM)
  about 12, 40, 95
  URL 12
Model View Whatever (MVW) 40
MonoDevelop 126
MonoDroid 126
MonoTouch 126

Moonlight 126
multiplayer games
  playing 4, 5
MVVM
  about 137
  chat 155, 156
  ChatHub 146-148
  ChatRooms 153-155
  DelegateCommand 139, 144
  login screen 148-152
  Messenger 138, 139
  security 144-146

N

network traffic
  analyzing 177
Ninject 97, 100, 110
NServiceBus 90
NuGet
  URL 16

O

observables 100, 101
Open Web Interface, for .NET 179

P

packages
  about 137
  setting up 24, 99, 100
patterns
  about 10
  Model View Controller (MVC)
      pattern 10, 11
  Model View ViewModel (MVVM) 12
  URL 10
PCL (Portable Class Library) 144
performance counters 172-176
persistent connections
  defining 21
principles and patterns
  URL 8
project
  code, defining 28, 29
  creating 22, 23

PropertyChanged 100
proxies 42-45
publish/subscribe 7

R

RabbitMQ support
  creating 90
Redis
  about 86
  URL 86
Remote Procedure Call (RPC) 38

S

scope 27
security
  adding 102
  client security service, creating 105-107
  defining 69
  helper, binding 103-105
  login view, adding 107-110
  support, adding for cookies 102
self-hosting
  about 179, 180
  client 184-186
  code, adding for 181-183
  packages, adding 180
separation 47
server
  defining 3
server-side
  defining 30
  dots, connecting 31, 32
  UI, creating 33-35
SignalR
  defining 6, 83, 84
  messages, defining 83, 84
single page application 25-28
Single Responsibility Principle
  about 9
  using 97
singletons 55
SOLID 8

SOLID, in programming
  URL 42
sources, logging
  defining 162
specific groups
  obtaining 49-54
stateful
  client 65, 66
  defining 63, 64
  lifetime event handlers 67
Strict Contextual Escaping (SCE) 55

T

terminal 2
tools
  about 15
  NuGet 16-18
  Visual Studio 2013 15
Twitter Bootstrap
  URL 15

U

UI
  composing 54-61

W

web application
  building, from HTML files 70
Web project
  setting 158, 159
**Windows Presentation Foundation
    (WPF) 126**

X

Xamarin Forms
  about 127
  URL 127
Xamarin Studio 126

Thank you for buying
SignalR – Real-time Application Development
Second Edition

About Packt Publishing

Packt, pronounced 'packed', published its first book, *Mastering phpMyAdmin for Effective MySQL Management*, in April 2004, and subsequently continued to specialize in publishing highly focused books on specific technologies and solutions.

Our books and publications share the experiences of your fellow IT professionals in adapting and customizing today's systems, applications, and frameworks. Our solution-based books give you the knowledge and power to customize the software and technologies you're using to get the job done. Packt books are more specific and less general than the IT books you have seen in the past. Our unique business model allows us to bring you more focused information, giving you more of what you need to know, and less of what you don't.

Packt is a modern yet unique publishing company that focuses on producing quality, cutting-edge books for communities of developers, administrators, and newbies alike. For more information, please visit our website at www.packtpub.com.

About Packt Open Source

In 2010, Packt launched two new brands, Packt Open Source and Packt Enterprise, in order to continue its focus on specialization. This book is part of the Packt Open Source brand, home to books published on software built around open source licenses, and offering information to anybody from advanced developers to budding web designers. The Open Source brand also runs Packt's Open Source Royalty Scheme, by which Packt gives a royalty to each open source project about whose software a book is sold.

Writing for Packt

We welcome all inquiries from people who are interested in authoring. Book proposals should be sent to author@packtpub.com. If your book idea is still at an early stage and you would like to discuss it first before writing a formal book proposal, then please contact us; one of our commissioning editors will get in touch with you.

We're not just looking for published authors; if you have strong technical skills but no writing experience, our experienced editors can help you develop a writing career, or simply get some additional reward for your expertise.

SignalR: Real-time Application Development

ISBN: 978-1-78216-424-1   Paperback: 124 pages

Utilize real-time functionality in your .NET applications with ease

1. Develop real-time applications across numerous platforms.

2. Create scalable applications that are ready for cloud deployment.

3. Utilize the full potential of SignalR.

SignalR Real-time Application Cookbook

ISBN: 978-1-78328-595-2   Paperback: 292 pages

Use SignalR to create real-time, bidirectional, and asynchronous applications based on standard web technologies

1. Build high performance real-time web applications.

2. Broadcast messages from the server to many clients simultaneously.

3. Implement complex and reactive architectures.

Please check **www.PacktPub.com** for information on our titles

SignalR Blueprints

ISBN: 978-1-78398-312-4   Paperback: 244 pages

Build real-time ASP.NET web applications with SignalR and create various interesting projects to improve your user experience

1. Learn how to apply real-time communications to your application.

2. Understand high-level concepts such as high frequency messaging with SignalR.

3. A step-by-step guide with real-world examples to help you develop applications.

Building Web Applications with Spring MVC [Video]

ISBN: 978-1-78328-653-9   Duration: 03:13 hours

Build dynamic and powerful server-side web applications in Java using Spring MVC

1. Implement Spring MVC controllers that handle user requests, return HTML responses, and handle errors.

2. Provide locale and theme support for web applications as well as build sturdy RESTful web services.

3. A practical guide that demonstrates building Spring MVC applications using an example of an online e-commerce chocolate store.

www.ingramcontent.com/pod-product-compliance
Lightning Source LLC
Chambersburg PA
CBHW060554060326

40690CB00017B/3705